DK
4348
.P8
C65
1996

Collins, David R.

Casimir Pulaski.

$14.95

DATE			

BAKER & TAYLOR

CASIMIR PULASKI

CASIMIR PULASKI

SOLDIER ON HORSEBACK

DAVID R. COLLINS

ILLUSTRATED BY
LARRY NOLTE

PELICAN PUBLISHING COMPANY
GRETNA 1996

Library of Congress Cataloging-in-Publication Data

Collins, David R.
    Casimir Pulaski : soldier on horseback / by David R. Collins ;
illustrated by Larry Nolte.
      p. cm.
    Includes bibliographical references and index.
    Summary: Presents the life of the American Revolutionary War
hero who was born in Poland and whose marble bust graces the
Capitol Rotunda in Washington, D.C.
    ISBN 1-56554-082-4 (alk. paper)
    1. Pulaski, Kazimierz, 1747-1779—Juvenile literature.
2. Generals—Poland—Biography—Juvenile literature. 3. Generals—
United States—Biography—Juvenile literature. 4. United States—
History—Revolution, 1775-1783—Participation, Polish—Juvenile
literature. [1. Pulaski, Kazimierz, 1747-1779. 2. Generals.
3. United States—History—Revolution, 1775-1783.] I. Nolte,
Larry, ill. II. Title.
DK4348.P8C65 1995
973.7'092—dc20
[b]
                                      95-34383
                                          CIP
                                          AC

Manufactured in the United States of America
Published by Pelican Publishing Company, Inc.
1101 Monroe Street, Gretna, Louisiana 70053

Contents

Preface

Recently, two hundred high school students in Illinois were asked a question: "What did Casimir Pulaski do?" It seemed a legitimate question to ask the Illinois young people since the first Monday in March is labeled "Pulaski Day" and the school doors remained closed. Most students offered no answer. Only seven of those students could identify Casimir Pulaski as a Revolutionary War hero. Twice as many identified him as an inventor, ten thought he was a composer, while one student said, "How should I know? I didn't even know he was in this class!"

Those Illinois high school students need not hang their heads in shame. Chances are, most Americans could not identify the contributions of Casimir Pulaski. Yet current reference data reveals one hundred and seventy-six counties, cities, towns, and bridges that carry the surname Pulaski. It's a major road in Chicago, a national monument on Cockspur Island in Georgia, and a marble bust in the Capitol Rotunda in Washington, D.C. For a man whose name appears across this nation in one way or another, Casimir Pulaski is rather a "mystery man" of American history.

George Washington certainly knew who Casimir Pulaski was. "He was the most noble kind of hero," observed the leader of the Continental Army during the Revolutionary

War and our nation's first president. "It is one thing to fight and to die for your country. It is quite another to fight and die for freedom itself. Americans should remember with great affection and gratitude the name Casimir Pulaski and his contributions. He was truly a man of courage and virtue."

Well, when a man the likes of George Washington feels someone should be remembered, I am inclined to agree. He was usually right when it came to judging people.

And as one who has taught for more than thirty years, in Illinois of all places, I pass along anything I learn that might better the lives of my students. Sometimes it is in my English classroom. Other times I reach farther, perhaps in a biography I choose to write.

So whether you are from Moline, Illinois, or Los Angeles, California, or Baltimore, Maryland, settle in for an adventure. In the pages that follow, you will meet Casimir Pulaski, the brave and daring soldier on horseback.

George Washington would be proud of you.

So will I.

CASIMIR PULASKI

Chapter One

"An Able Horseman"

In the early 1700s, the country of Poland sat like a contented mouse, full of the foodstuffs grown and harvested on its own fertile farmlands. Unfortunately, two hungry "cats" roamed along its borders. To Poland's west lurked Prussia, later to become Germany. To the east prowled Russia, a sprawling major power. Both of these countries eyed Poland with interest, eager to control its seacoast along the Baltic Sea, its rich farmlands, as well as its energetic people.

While the two cats licked their lips at the thought of taking over Poland, the proud people of the country went about their business. War was far from their minds, but those who feared its eventual arrival were not about to give up their country and their freedom without a fight.

Joseph Pulaski had much more than his freedom to lose. The shrewd lawyer had made fine use of his legal skills. Often he chose to be paid in land rather than money. The rich landowner accumulated whole villages and towns in payment for his services, or sometimes he took over handsome farms and fields.

The Pulaski family estate was among the finest homesteads in all Poland. Called "The Winiary," the family home sat on a hillside overlooking the Vistula River. Tall white columns lined the front of the house and shone in the afternoon sun. Handsome bushes and trees, carefully trimmed, dotted the surrounding landscape. Inside the sprawling house, servants bustled, tending to the needs of the owner's family.

It was into such a world that Casimir Pulaski was born on March 4, 1747. As the second son of Joseph Pulaski, young Casimir enjoyed the pleasures of wealth without responsibilities. It was the eldest son, Casimir's brother, Francis, who would someday inherit the family land and riches. Therefore, Francis received the lion's share of attention, while his two younger brothers and five younger sisters escaped notice.

There was an old Polish legend that if a baby cried loudly at baptism, he was shouting away the devil. Baptisms in the Pulaski family were held in the family chapel at the rear of the house. Gold trim lined the white walls, while rosy-cheeked angels played among clouds painted on the ceiling. As the water trickled down tiny Casimir's pink forehead, it was said he let out a deafening cry. The crowd smiled, grateful for the good sign.

Joseph Pulaski firmly believed when a child was old enough to walk, he was old enough to ride. His son Casimir's first memory of childhood was his father plopping him into a saddle atop a pony. With quick hands and steady movement, the man led his son down the sandy driveway of Winiary. To the gate of the closest village they went and then returned. By the time the trip was over, Joseph Pulaski declared Casimir "an able horseman, worthy of the Pulaski name." The child was too young to know what that meant. But he soon discovered riding lessons played an important part of each day.

At five, Casimir received a horse of his own. It was a hand-me-down from his older brother Francis, and it was a pony rather than a horse. But it did not matter to Casimir. He was as proud of his pony as Francis was of the fine Arabian mare he now rode over the Winiary grounds.

But Joseph Pulaski was not content with any of his

eight children just being able to ride. Riding was an art—a talent for display. The old stable coachman Michael shared that thinking. Each Pulaski child became Michael's student. Cantering, galloping, trotting—all riding skills were mastered.

Once Casimir was able to ride with speed and precision, Michael added shooting to the lessons. It was almost as important for a Pulaski to be a good hunter as a good horseman. Hunting demanded one hand on the bridle and one on the gun. There were times when both hands needed to be free for shooting. Then, it was the knees that would guide the horse. One almost needed to be a skilled acrobat to handle both riding and shooting at the same time.

Yet that is exactly what Casimir did! Under Michael's skilled supervision, the boy learned to handle a gun and reins with speed and precision. But what about those times when the hunter needed to shoot while his horse needed to jump? What of riding along narrow paths while shooting— or fording a gushing stream? Michael took his young student through every possible situation. The coachman set high standards. It was not enough merely to do something, according to the old stableman. It had to be done well. Joseph Pulaski supported Michael's thoughts and teaching. The proud father looked on with pride as he watched Casimir ride and shoot with skill and ease.

Not that schoolwork was ignored. At six, Casimir headed off to the parish school nearby which his brothers and sisters also attended. Thanks to his mother, the boy already knew the basics of reading and writing when he started classes. Now Latin appeared on his list of studies. The boy pursued his schoolwork with energy. Yet his papers and tests seldom revealed the highest marks. It was clear that Casimir Pulaski enjoyed the fun and games after classes more than schoolwork.

"To the woods!" someone would call.

It took only a moment for the students to mount their

horses and become make-believe soldiers. Apples on fences, saplings, and tree stumps became the enemy. The boys practiced their shooting. When they tired of that, they carved wooden lances. Through the pockets of trees they galloped on horseback, thrusting their long lances into bushes and shrubs. On windy days the young soldiers tied light boards to hanging branches. The targets swayed in the breeze.

"Charge!"

The call for attack brought the boys, whooping and hollering, racing toward their imaginary enemies. The lances speared the boards, shattering them into small pieces. Each contact raised a louder cheer, a victory yell. It was strange play in a country that had not seen battle or bloodshed in over one hundred years. Yet someday these games played in a Polish woods would take on usefulness and meaning—especially for young Casimir Pulaski.

Chapter Two

The Mysterious Stranger

The Polish people felt safe and secure throughout Casimir's childhood. The richest of families kept their doors unlocked at night. After all, there was nothing to fear. Even the hungry beggar roaming the streets was welcomed into any Polish home. "The guest in the home is Christ in the home," people would say. Poland, being heavily Catholic, treated guests with kindness.

No one took hospitality more seriously than Joseph Pulaski. He entertained often, inviting family and friends into the Winiary for overnight visits or stays of many weeks. The poor man was made just as welcome as the rich man. A loaf of bread sat waiting in the Winiary pantry for any unexpected stranger, while a kettle of hot soup brewed nearby.

Casimir passed through his earliest years learning such customs. The tall muscular youth, whose shoulder-length hair usually lay tousled from riding, was a favorite among Winiary servants. They spoke of the boy's good manners and cheerfulness. He took few advantages as the master's son. Now and then a few extra tarts or biscuits would disappear from the pantry shelf, but nothing more than that.

Casimir's conduct pleased Joseph Pulaski. He wanted no spoiled children and worked hard to see that he had none. Marianne, his wife, kept a close watch on her daughters, making sure they acquired the proper manners of young

15

women born to wealth and position. They learned how to plan meals and sew, how to arrange flowers and sing songs. But the mistress of the house also wanted no snobbery, no affectation. Casimir's five sisters learned courtesy and respect. They made frequent trips to the shrines of Our Lady of Czestochowa which lined the country's roads. The girls laid flowers before the tiny stone statues of the Lord's mother who reached out to bless travelers on their journeys.

Like his father, Casimir hoped to become a lawyer. But he saw something more in his father. Joseph Pulaski was a listener and a thinker. People brought their problems to him, and he found solutions. Often Casimir would sneak into the study where his father welcomed business guests. Unnoticed, the boy would curl up on the floor beneath the giant wooden table to listen to the discussions taking place. Although there was no fighting in Poland, there could be arguments and angry disagreements. Joseph Pulaski had a way of listening to all sides and then offering an opinion that would pull the conflicting parties together. Casimir marveled at his father's wisdom. Often the boy heard his father called "a great statesman."

But Casimir's greatest love was riding or spending time in the Winiary stables with the horses. He knew every mare and colt. More than one visitor mistook Casimir for a stable boy. He shunned the fancy linen jackets and breeches worn by most of his position. He preferred the tough leather and flax clothing worn by the servants. He did their work too, cheerfully feeding the horses, washing them down, and combing their manes. There was no task too small or too unimportant as long as it involved the horses.

As Casimir approached his eighth birthday, he hoped he would receive a graceful and sleek Arabian mare like his brother had received. If it was a matter of riding skill, Casimir knew he would get a horse. Michael said the boy rode better than any student he had ever taught.

The boy rose early the morning of March 4, 1755. He

barely took time to dress himself before heading to the stable. Quickly he ran from stall to stall, eagerly searching for a new addition.

Then from outside, there came a loud whinny. Casimir dashed to the stable door. Michael sat smiling on the back of a golden stallion. He joked something about finding the horse roaming alone on the Winiary grounds.

Casimir knew the truth. He could hardly wait for the coachman to climb down. Then Casimir boarded the horse and raced ahead, the wind biting into his face and tossing his hair as he flew over the Winiary grounds. The rider and his steed were friends at once, challenging the land beneath them.

Each morning Casimir started the day with a ride on his new horse. But a few days later as the boy left the house to go to the stables, a strange event occurred, a story he told all his life.

A light snow coated the ground, softening Casimir's steps. In the early morning darkness, the boy made out the outline of a figure leaning against the cookhouse.

"Let Jesus Christ be praised," Casimir said. It was a common greeting to beggars.

"For endless ages, amen," answered the stranger. His voice was weak, his head drooped. Clearly the man was tired.

Reaching inside his pocket, Casimir felt two coins, one gold and the other silver. They had been birthday gifts. The boy handed the gold coin to the man, then ran to the cookhouse door. He banged on the door. Where was the cook? Casimir wondered. Was he stirring the coals or mixing batter for biscuits? Finally, a face appeared at the doorway. The door opened just a crack.

Casimir pulled the door open. "Quick! There is a man out here who needs food."

The boy turned and led the way to where the beggar had been standing. But there was no one in sight.

"But he stood in this very spot!" Casimir insisted. "Look there on the snowy ground. You can still see his footprints!"

Sure enough, the prints were there. It was as if the man had taken flight from where he stood. Casimir shook his head. Had he been dreaming?

Quickly the boy fished into his pocket. He pulled out the silver coin. The gold coin was missing.

Later, Casimir told his story to his father. The man shook his head. "Perhaps, just perhaps, you have met Jesus Christ. It is said He roams in the form of a beggar. You treated this man with kindness. Perhaps you have brought safety to our home."

Casimir smiled. He knew he would never forget the meeting with the stranger.

But as to the safety of the Pulaski home, there were already plans taking place that would disturb that safety. The "cats" that prowled along the country's borders grew hungrier. The rich, contented "mouse" that was Poland was soon to become too appetizing for the nations around it.

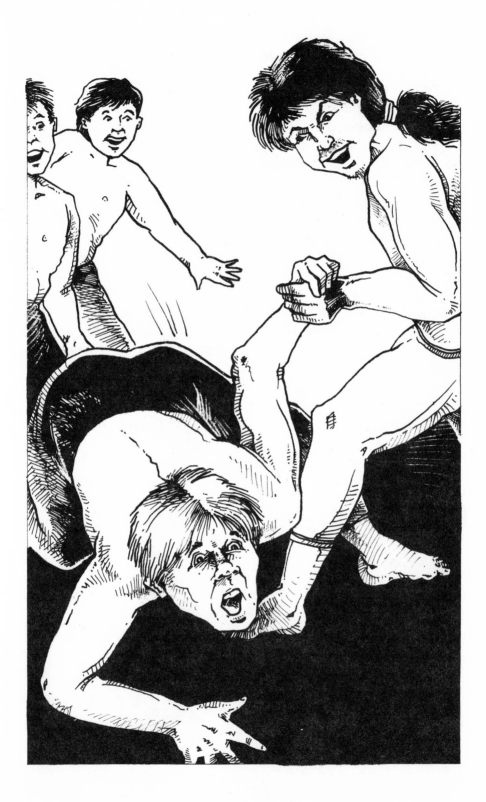

Chapter Three

Dark Shadows

Joseph Pulaski spent more and more time away from Winiary. Often he traveled to Warsaw, Poland's capital, to attend meetings. Other times he went to diets, gatherings of officials from local governments around the country. The diets were very important to the running of Poland. They elected the king, made laws, and set taxes.

As the owner of eight villages and towns, as well as over one hundred farms, Joseph Pulaski had business across the entire country. Sometimes he was gone for weeks at a time. The sight of his father's carriage rolling toward the Winiary always brought Casimir galloping on horseback as fast as he could. Men often came to the house while the respected lawyer was home. Talks lasted long into the night. At times loud shouts came from the study. Often the word "Cossacks" thundered inside the stone walls of the big house.

As Casimir grew older, he heard more and more about the Cossacks. Pirates on horseback they were, swooping down from Russia and raiding small villages. No one ever seemed to know where or when they would strike next.

A confused Casimir Pulaski asked his father about the evil Cossacks. Why couldn't the Polish army stop the bandits?

The answer was simple. The Polish army had become too weak. At one time the army boasted thousands of trained soldiers. Other nations in Europe, threatened by aggressors, often called upon Poland for help.

But the long reign of peace in Poland and the shorter reign of King Augustus III had changed all that. Poles felt safe and secure. Most people felt there was little need for huge collections of troops. Now men served as guards of honor for rich noblemen and landlords. As honor guards, the men wore fancy uniforms and rode fine horses. Although considered soldiers, these men knew little of shooting, fencing, or any military training. King Augustus III paid no attention to maintaining a strong national army. He was interested in the arts—music, painting, sculpture, and poetry. In the royal palace the sounds of the Cossacks' invading hoofbeats were drowned out by the strains of traveling minstrels singing ballads.

But Joseph Pulaski's ears were tuned to the increasing attacks of Russian bandits. Each town he visited in northern Poland carried tales of another Cossack assault. He traveled across the country, urging the diets to help build a national Polish army. Few people listened. A bigger army meant increased taxes. Rich Polish businessmen poured their money into new industries and trade. Many leaders felt that if Poland built up its army, so would other countries. Some foreign leader would then want to put that army to work in a war. Most people agreed that Poland should just remain at peace.

"Russia is already building up its army," warned Pulaski.

"To catch the Cossack thieves!" came the answer. No one would even think that Russia might be building an army to attack Poland.

Joseph Pulaski simply shook his head. Why would no one listen?

Yet there was someone who *would* listen. Ten-year-old Casimir heard every word his father spoke. He sat with his father at dinner when guests visited. The long wooden table was often surrounded by twenty or thirty people at a time. Casimir listened to each word spoken, then walked with the group into the study where the conversation continued.

Father Mark, the local Catholic priest, was also a frequent visitor to the Winiary. Every afternoon he chatted with the Pulaskis over coffee, then led vesper services in the chapel.

Most evenings, Casimir's mother entertained the family and guests with her musical talents. As she sang, her small nimble fingers flew across the keys of the harpsicord. Usually the slight, dark-haired woman chose happy songs— melodies that her eight children could also sing.

Yet Marianne Pulaski could be as determined as she was cheerful and carefree. With her husband gone so often, she supervised more and more of the running of Winiary. She hired servants, decided what crops to plant, and kept financial records. Casimir, his sisters and brothers, knew better than to interrupt their mother when she was busy.

On the other hand, Joseph Pulaski would interrupt whatever he was doing if one of his children wished his attention. Family came first, then business. But both Casimir and his brother Francis did all they could to shelter their father from distractions. At times their siblings resented their older brothers' actions. Yet arguing with them was useless.

For six years Casimir attended the local parish school. When he was twelve, he headed to Warsaw to attend high school. The Theatine priests ran the school, which emphasized writing, literature, the Latin classics, and arithmetic. Since he spent so much time in Warsaw, Joseph Pulaski owned a home in the city. During the daytime, he worked at his law practice while Casimir attended classes. At night, the two went to the homes of friends to dine. To Joseph

Pulaski, it was just as important for his children to learn good manners as it was to learn how to read and translate an essay written in Latin.

One night Casimir got a big surprise. His father took him to the palace of King Augustus III. Every wall in the royal house was dotted with grand paintings. Guards dressed in satin and lace uniforms herded the guests into a concert room where musicians played for two hours. Then it was on to the dining room. An oak table, seventy feet long, lay covered with handsome meats, fruits, breads and biscuits, cakes and pies. Candles blazed in crystal candelabra lining the walls and on top of the giant table. Casimir's eyes widened. Winiary was grand indeed, but it was nothing compared to all of this!

Casimir enjoyed life in Warsaw. Often, he struggled with his schoolwork. His father encouraged his efforts, but never demanded that he be the top student in his class. It was more important to Joseph Pulaski that his children love God, their family, and their country.

In the summer of 1762, Casimir moved on to his final school. At the court of the duke of Courland, fifteen-year-old Casimir would learn to be both a page and a soldier. Located on the Russian frontier near the Baltic Sea, Courland Castle was a month's traveling distance from Winiary.

At first, being so far from home proved difficult for young Casimir. Courland was a whole new world. Gone were the sounds of his laughing brothers and sisters, and of his mother's happy songs. Gone were the evenings with his father in Warsaw, the hours of political talk. Thankfully, there were a few boys there from school that he knew. But Casimir missed the chance to dress as a stable boy and jump on the back of a horse. At Courland, he wore linen shirts trimmed in lace, embroidered waistcoats, satin knee breeches, and flowered damask coats.

Casimir took a quick liking to the duke and duchess of Courland. Only a few years older than he, they treated him more like a friend than a page. Still, he learned all about court manners, including dancing, bowing, and how to make pleasant conversation. Casimir learned quickly, although he saw little need for creating idle chatter about fashion and fine foods.

Soldiering was more to Casimir's taste. His skill on horseback proved a quick advantage. Michael had taught him well at Winiary. Always a crack shot, Casimir learned speed and precision with a pistol. He learned how to handle a lance too, and was grateful for the earlier days of play in the woods with his schoolmates.

The duke's guards were tough teachers. It was not enough to know merely how to be a soldier *with* a weapon. It was important to know how to defend oneself *without* a pistol or lance.

Each soldier trainee learned how to wrestle. The muscles on Casimir's six-foot frame toughened, his shoulders grew thick and firm, and he turned and twisted quickly. He soon beat the other pages in competitions, then began wrestling the other guards. He chose to keep the mustache he grew, feeling it added years to his appearance.

Casimir cast off all feelings of homesickness. As weeks slipped into months, the young duke and duchess came to be like family to Casimir. The older guards recognized Casimir's skills on horseback, with a pistol and lance, or with his bare hands. Whenever he could, he visited the duke's library, poring over books of military victories and historical battles.

And then came that awful morning when Casimir awoke to loud noises outside his room. He recognized a few Russian words being shouted. Footsteps ran past his door. What was happening? the boy wondered. Was the castle under attack?

Chapter Four

Angry Voices

Terror was frozen on the faces of the duke and duchess of Courland when Casimir saw them. During the night Russian soldiers had surrounded and captured the castle. No, the invaders were not Cossacks. They were trained members of the Russian army.

To fifteen-year-old Casimir Pulaski, it all seemed like a bad dream. Why would anyone want Courland Castle? The duke and duchess were harmless. The few guards and pages were of threat to no one. Yet Casimir soon learned the castle was completely shut off from the outside world.

Joseph Pulaski was furious when he found out what had happened at Courland Castle. The angry lawyer called on King Augustus III, demanding immediate action. Calmly, the king promised to look into the matter.

A king's commissioner rode from Warsaw to Courland. "The situation is perilous," the official wrote back. "Request 2,000 troops at once."

King Augustus III paid little attention to the request. Instead of two thousand soldiers, the ruler sent forty.

Meanwhile, the prisoners of Courland Castle pondered their future, if indeed they had one. Although the Russians promised no violence, Casimir was unsure if their word was good. The Russian commander made no attempt to hide his feelings about his Polish prisoners. He made fun of the duke and duchess, calling them names and forcing them to eat from the scraps his men left behind on their plates.

Day after day Casimir awaited rescue. Surely the king would not allow invaders from another country to take over a Polish fort without a fight. Such a thing had never happened before in all history!

Yet that is exactly what happened. King Augustus III saw no purpose in going to war, even for such an important place at Courland Castle. The duke and duchess were ordered to return to Warsaw with their belongings. Casimir packed his things and left with them.

It was a long, sad journey. Word of the incident traveled quickly across the Polish countryside. People stood silent along the road watching the caravan of wagons pass by. There were no words exchanged, yet the silence spoke a sad tale. The faces of the people looked tired and confused. Why was this happening? How could it be? What had happened to the strong and noble Poland they loved?

Casimir could find few words of comfort to share with the duke and duchess when they parted in Warsaw. He was so grateful for the time he had spent with them. How kind they had been. Yet, it had ended in such an ugly way.

So often Casimir had greeted his father upon his return to Winiary. Now it was the father who greeted the son. The lawyer stood on the front steps of the sprawling family home. His arms opened to hug Casimir as soon as the boy leaped off his horse.

To Joseph Pulaski, Russia's plans were clear. Bit by bit the hungry "cat" would gobble up slices of Poland. Courland was just the beginning. A strong national Polish army needed to be formed. There was not a moment to waste.

News of the death of King Augustus III cast a shadow of gloom across the country. Yet Joseph Pulaski also saw it as a chance to strengthen the nation. A diet would be called to elect a new king. Surely, with what had happened in Courland, the new king would call for a build-up of the Polish army.

Joseph Pulaski and his three sons, Francis, Casimir, and Anthony, packed their bags, climbed into a coach, and headed to Warsaw. Across the nation, thirty-five thousand electors also streamed toward the capital city. There were not enough rooms in Warsaw to house all the visitors. A giant tent city sprang up along the nearby hillside. Banners snapped in the breeze, each flag displaying the coat of arms of a different Polish family.

Joseph Pulaski made it no secret whom he supported as the new king of Poland. The duke of Courland was a clear choice. Young and level-headed, he had always shown signs of becoming a wise and noble leader. Having lost his castle to the ruthless Russians, what better fate than to find a new home in the king's palace?

But there were many who feared Pulaski's choice. Would not the duke of Courland seek immediate revenge for the actions taken against him? Surely Poland would go to war at once.

Another candidate emerged. Stanislaus Augustus Poniatowski was almost a duplicate copy of the dead king. Another lover of the arts, he enjoyed grand music, literature, and paintings. Not only did he love the arts, he had also won the affection of Empress Catherine of Russia. The shrewd Russian monarch let it be known that any Pole voting for Poniatowski would be richly rewarded.

Hearing of Empress Catherine's actions, Joseph Pulaski was outraged. He publicly declared that "a Pole's honor cannot be bought." But money spoke louder than Pulaski. When the votes for king were cast in 1764, Poniatowski was elected. It was a discouraged Joseph Pulaski who returned to Winiary with his three sons.

Sending the new Polish king out to enjoy his concerts and art exhibits, the Russian ambassador in Warsaw set an evil series of plans in motion. Always the Catholic people of Poland enjoyed a strong allegiance to their spiritual leader in Rome. The pope's power and decisions gave direction to

Polish lives. Repnin, the Russian ambassador, knew that bond had to be broken. Carefully, he schemed and met with his helpers. He wrote up a new government bill that would set up two religious parties in Poland—Roman Catholic and Eastern Orthodox. Those people following the Eastern Orthodox beliefs would receive many privileges.

Poles, devoted to their Roman Catholic faith, protested the new bill. Across the country they held diets in which they voted to censure the king for allowing such a bill to be proposed. Joseph Pulaski, his sons Francis and Casimir standing beside him, spoke out clearly against the king's action at the diet held outside Warsaw. The Catholic Church and its laws were accepted as the governing force of Poland.

The Russian ambassador was delighted. The actions of the Polish leaders fell right into his plan. He quickly informed other European leaders that Poland had no religious freedom. Protestants and members of Orthodox faiths were destined for persecution. Always England, Sweden, Holland, and other European nations had respected Poland. Now, as rumors of planned executions and torture circulated, the foreign countries were outraged. Leaders protested the actions of the Polish diets. Ambassador Repnin sent word to his friends in the Warsaw parliament. He told them to condemn the diets and to ask the Russian army to help keep order in Poland.

Joseph Pulaski saw through the Repnin scheme. If the Russians were invited to enter Poland, they would never leave. They might even claim the country as their own.

At about this same time, a letter reached Winiary. The members of Parliament in Warsaw summoned Joseph Pulaski to appear within four days before government officials. If he failed to do so, he would be breaking the law.

Casimir accompanied his father to the Great Convention Hall on Sigismund Square in Warsaw in the fall of 1766. He sat in the gallery watching the Parliament officials on the floor below. Tension was in the air. Joseph Pulaski was ordered forward. One by one, Ambassador Repnin's friends accused Pulaski of stirring up the diets across the nation. "You have turned your countrymen into traitors!" one official shouted.

Joseph Pulaski gripped the chair in which he sat. His jawbone remained rigid, his face reddening in rage. Finally, he could take no more. He jumped to his feet.

"If there is treason in this land, it is not with me. It is with the Russian ambassador who would bring his country's troops into our peace-loving nation." The lawyer stopped a moment, catching his breath. "We Poles love liberty. We will give our lives to stay free. And I would challenge the Russian ambassador to a duel at any time if he chooses to question my love for Poland."

The words stunned those listening. Casimir wanted to stand up and cheer his father. Quickly a group of Joseph Pulaski's friends surrounded him and escorted him out of the hall. Challenging a foreign ambassador was a dangerous thing to do.

In the days that followed, the halls of Winiary hummed with whispers. What would the new Polish king do about Joseph Pulaski? It was clear that Russia had gained a great deal of influence. Would the king punish Joseph Pulaski for his challenge to duel? Perhaps the lawyer might be put to death. It was a thought that caused young Casimir Pulaski many sleepless nights. To the nineteen-year-old boy, his father was a hero, a symbol of courage and wisdom. No one loved Poland more than Joseph Pulaski. Casimir was sure of that. Yet the young man hoped that his father's love would not bring a death sentence.

Chapter Five

"The Guerilla Colonel"

Days slipped into weeks. Weeks became months. No word about the fate of Joseph Pulaski came from the palace. King Stanislaus Augustus Poniatowski seemed too busy buying new paintings and commissioning new writers to do anything to save his people from their enemies. The new Polish monarch appeared to be totally unconcerned about freedom in his country. Quietly, Russian soldiers crossed the border, keeping their ears open for Poles who might resist.

The neighboring nations of France and Austria watched developments in Poland closely. Russia appeared too eager to spread itself outside its own boundaries. If Poland were to fall, who would be next?

Early in 1767, Joseph Pulaski decided to scheme a bit himself. He was not about to let Russia take over Poland without a fight. If the Polish king and his government would not raise an army, Pulaski would. No soldier himself, his three sons, Francis, twenty-one, Casimir, nineteen, and Anthony, fourteen, stood ready to help. Each had been well trained as a horseman and a skilled marksman. All the Pulaskis met in the family chapel at Winiary, bowed their heads, and prayed with Father Mark. Out of that gathering came the birth of the Knights of the Holy Cross.

It was fortunate that Joseph Pulaski owned farms across Poland. Some could be kept as military bases, shelters for young men to train as soldiers. Those joining the Knights of the Holy Cross were expected to bring their own equipment and pay their own expenses. For those who could not afford those expenses, the elder Pulaski planned to sell some of his farms and farmlands. Freedom, he knew, would not be free.

Joseph assigned each of his sons to a different location in the country. Little attention would be paid to the Pulaski sons traveling to various territories. People would think they were visiting the family farms to check on the crops and equipment. After all, they would soon be taking over their father's investments.

Casimir headed east. He stopped and spread the word in every village and farmhouse. Anyone wishing to join a resistance effort against the Russians should come and learn the skills of soldiering. He cautioned the volunteers to come alone, not in groups. Men traveling in numbers might arouse suspicion.

The plan worked well. Casimir welcomed each man as he arrived. Training began at once. Riding, shooting, wrestling—every skill Casimir had learned he taught to the men coming in. He passed along all the military tactics he had read about at the Winiary and the duke's castle.

While Casimir trained soldiers, Francis collected money and supplies from rich landlords and nobles. If a revolt should come, he told the people, it would be costly. A hefty treasury was needed.

A trickle of trained warriors became a stream, then a rushing wave. Six became six hundred, then six thousand. Word of the resistance movement swept the country. Casimir knew that any moment he could be seized and put to death as a traitor.

At first, the headquarters of the Knights of the Holy Cross moved around. It was too dangerous to stay in one place. The small town of Bar seemed a good spot to remain. It housed a religious shrine which attracted many Catholic pilgrims. No one would suspect people coming into and leaving the area, which was far out in the country.

Finally, Joseph Pulaski called for a full meeting of the troops. Almost six thousand men heard him read a manifesto of freedom. The document was not merely aimed at Poland. The lawyer called upon all nations "to witness the obligation which bound the Poles to repel by arms, if need be, the foreign yoke placed on a free, independent nation by the Empress of Russia." The assembled Knights of the Holy Cross listened to every word. Casimir stood rigid, his lean face watching his father's every move. Joseph Pulaski continued, calling upon Poland "to arise, to postpone every other consideration but that of resisting tyranny."

The document touched the hearts of the assembled men. They cheered their agreement and approval.

Yet it was not Joseph Pulaski's intent merely to arouse the emotions of the group. He wanted them to think about their cause, their reasons for action. In the days that followed, he saw that the men took a solemn vow to defend Poland and the Catholic Church. "Never let it be said that we would persecute anyone for their religion," he said. Father Mark led the men in prayer. Casimir pledged that he would never again consider his own comfort or safety. He promised that he would give his life, whenever needed, for his God and for freedom.

Across Poland, more and more resistance movements formed. Hoping to avoid bloodshed, Joseph Pulaski publicly ordered the Russian soldiers to leave Polish soil. "Return to us what is ours," the lawyer demanded.

The answer came in the form of eight thousand Russian soldiers, sent to end "this revolt against the King." News of their march into Poland traveled from farm to farm. Casimir Pulaski did not waste a moment when he heard about the advancing troops. Putting together a small company of soldiers, he rode out to scout the Russian army.

Unexpectedly, Casimir and his men ran head-on into the

Russians. The well-trained Poles opened fire, their shots hitting the moving targets. Casimir had prepared his men well. The confused Russian soldiers dove for cover, thinking they were under attack by a mighty enemy force. The Russian bugler sounded retreat. Russians scrambled out of the line of fire. The Knights of the Holy Cross cheered their victory.

Casimir felt proud of his men. Greatly outnumbered, they had beaten the enemy. After that battle, Casimir dubbed himself "the guerilla colonel." He continued leading his men on surprise raids against the Russians, then slipping into the dark Polish forests.

Usually, the Polish troops numbered in the hundreds while the Russian soldiers came in thousands. Casimir thrived on such odds. It challenged his resourcefulness.

In the summer of 1769, the Russians thought they had cornered Poland's "guerilla colonel." They chased Casimir into a swamp. But the young Polish leader recalled a similar campaign he had read about at Courland. Quickly he helped his men build a bridge over the muck and mire of the swamp. They managed to escape, leaving the Russians confused and frustrated.

But leaders of the Polish resistance had special plans for Casimir. They dispatched him with a troop of soldiers to protect the Burdyczow Monastery. The old fortress housed all the gold collected to back the cause of the Knights of the Holy Cross.

The dilapidated monastery sat atop a bluff, a river curving behind it. Once situated inside, Casimir knew it was a dangerous position. The Russians could surround the fort and simply hold its residents prisoner. Without food and provisions, it would be merely a matter of time before the Poles would starve.

The Russians did exactly that. Now and then they moved forward, hurling shots at the men inside. Both sides suffered casualties, but the Russians replaced their injured men with fresh troops. Casimir had no such opportunity to bring in replacements. Gradually, food and water ran out. The monks still living in the fort begged Pulaski to surrender.

Casimir firmly refused. After all, he had pledged to give his life for freedom. Only twenty, he was ready to sacrifice his life for his God and his freedom. He had no thought of giving up, of quitting. It ran against everything he believed.

But the sight of dying men and the pleas of the monks of Burdyczow around him broke the young man's spirit. The monks were God's special servants. Should he, a mere soldier, not listen to these men of great faith? If it was only his own life at risk, it would be different. Sadly, he ordered the white flag of surrender hoisted above the fort's walls. The Russians advanced and took their prisoners. They seized all the donations of the patriotic Poles who were eager to support the Knights of the Holy Cross.

From his position at Bar, headquarters of the Knights, Joseph Pulaski received sad news. A messenger brought word that all three of his sons had been killed. The Russians were already on their way to his location. If Francis, Casimir, and Anthony were gone, surely they were with God. Their father was certain of that. Convinced they had died bravely in the service of their Maker and for their country, Joseph Pulaski readied his Knights for enemy attack.

On the outside of the city stood raised ramparts on every side. Joseph Pulaski placed himself where he could view the proceedings. The Russian soldiers set up cannons and positioned themselves facing the city.

Suddenly a figure appeared at the front rampart. It was Father Mark, carrying a crucifix. "In the name of God, in the name of a free Poland, put down your weapons," the man of God said.

The Russians paid no attention. They shifted a giant cannon into position and loaded it. Yet as the cannon fired, it exploded in the midst of Russian soldiers.

It was a miracle Joseph Pulaski shouted.

The Polish monks and churchmen inside the city agreed. Bravely they offered to go and meet the Russian leaders in an effort to bring a peaceful settlement. Joseph Pulaski consented.

Shortly after sunrise, a stream of men poured out of Bar. They wore their uniforms of faith, evident to the Russians facing the city. Unarmed except for the crucifixes they carried, the priests wore faces of hope and trust.

The early morning air roared with the crackle of Russian guns. The priests, gasping their final breaths, slumped to the ground. From his viewing position, Joseph Pulaski stood horrified. His top aides surrounded him, urging him to flee. If the enemy would kill priests, they would kill anyone.

Pulaski knew his men were right. Rounding up the diet leaders who had supported the cause of Polish freedom, he led them from the city. The Turkish border twenty miles away promised safety.

King Stanislaus declared the uprising ended. But there were many in the country who felt no joy at the news. The stories of Joseph Pulaski and his sons lifted them to hero status. Casimir, especially, became the people's champion, as tales of his brave fighting spread from village to village. The story of how he defeated two thousand Russians with only four hundred brave Knights was told often. And then it became four thousand Russians against two hundred Poles. Or perhaps it was six thousand Russians and a handful of patriots. "The guerilla colonel" became more courageous and noble with each story told.

Wanting to ensure that Casimir would never fight again, the Russians urged him to sign a pledge of peace. Risking death, the twenty-year-old "guerilla colonel" refused. The Russians knew they dared not kill their captive. The entire country was under his spell. News of Casimir's execution could cause another revolution. Yet they had to get rid of him and their other prisoners.

Finally, the Russians banished Casimir and his brothers to Turkey. Since their father was there, it appeared like a kind gesture. The Russians wanted no more trouble from the Pulaskis. "Stay out of Poland!" they were told.

It was a foolish hope. Even as Casimir crossed into Turkey, he promised to return to his beloved Poland.

Chapter Six

Hailing a Hero

Joseph Pulaski joyfully greeted his sons. For the man who had once been told that all three of his boys were dead, the reunion brought tears of celebration.

But there was no time to waste. Every day of Russian occupation of Poland angered Joseph Pulaski. Once again he made plans to free his country of the cruel intruders. Francis, Casimir, and Anthony stood ready to assist. Boldly, Joseph Pulaski rode back into Poland and issued a proclamation of freedom. He wanted loyal Poles to know that the cause of resistance was still alive. Then he returned to Turkey to regroup the Knights of the Holy Cross who had fled with him. Turkish officials worried about Joseph Pulaski's activities. They arrested him to prevent him causing trouble in their country.

The three Pulaski brothers remained in Poland. Francis rode from town to town, carrying the news of a fresh revolution. Casimir and Anthony took over two forts on the Dneiper River near the Turkish border. Here, they would train the young men who came to join the cause.

Just as Casimir and Anthony started training men, the Russians learned of their activities. Now at war against Turkey, the Russians persuaded the king of Poland that they needed protection. Otherwise, the Turkish troops might cross Poland and invade Russia. The Polish king gave the Russians the two forts on the Dnieper River. Quickly the Russians headed to the forts.

Anthony Pulaski rode out to scout the oncoming Russians. The enemy took the sixteen-year-old boy prisoner, carting him away to Siberia, a distant and desolate part of Russia used for captives. News of their brother's capture saddened Casimir and Francis. A few days later they heard that Anthony was dead. There was no time to grieve. The Russian soldiers were marching on the fort. Casimir wanted to stay and fight. But he knew it was hopeless.

As the enemy neared, Casimir took quick action. He rounded up his men, and with the help of an old gypsy guide, retreated on rocks behind the forts. Casimir glanced back to see the roofs of the two forts ablaze. In the darkness, he could not find Francis.

The next morning, the Russians fished many bodies out of the river. They hoped two of them were Francis and Casimir Pulaski. Were the Knights of the Holy Cross finished? The Russians prayed they were.

Casimir regrouped his forces and headed west to Cracow. A new army, the Polish Revolutionary Confederates, was gathering troops and arms to fight off the Russians. Casimir led his men across the treacherous Tatra Mountains. By the time they arrived at Cracow. the dwindling Knights of the Holy Cross were tired and hungry.

The Confederates wanted to avoid all-out warfare against the Russians. They urged France to join their cause. Perhaps, with the power of another mighty European nation behind them, the Confederates could peacefully persuade the Russian troops to leave.

Casimir joined in and helped to train new recruits. News that his brother, Francis, was alive and well rallied his spirits. He hurried to meet his brother on the plains beyond the Tatra Mountains.

Francis brought tragic news. He had located the Turkish prison in which their father was held, only to discover disease raging rampant there. Joseph Pulaski died in his dungeon cell, his last words a prayer to God for a free Poland. When Francis tried to take his father back to Winiary for burial, the Russians blocked his way. They took the body of Joseph Pulaski and left it on the open prairie.

Casimir could not hold back his tears. Many of his fighting friends wept too upon hearing of the death of Joseph Pulaski. Masses were held in his memory throughout Poland.

With new energy, Casimir and Francis promised to run the Russian soldiers out of the country. Leaving most of their troops in the old city of Sambor, they rode to Lithuania. This tiny Polish province had been overrun by Russians, and there were many native Lithuanians eager to form an opposing force.

Casimir rallied some four thousand young Lithuanians to serve. He drilled and trained the recruits in guerilla warfare. "Surprise attack is vital," he emphasized. "We must be prepared to catch the enemy off guard, then disappear into woods or swampland." These hit and run tactics Casimir knew well from the past. They worked beautifully, gradually cutting away at the size of Russian battalions. The Lithuanians captured giant ammunition stations, gaining both cannons and rifles. On July 6, 1769, Casimir led a victory charge against the main Russian army positioned at Kukielki. What was left of the foreign intruders trudged home to Russia.

"Hail to Casimir Pulaski!"

Poles cheered their new hero everywhere he went. At twenty-two, Casimir Pulaski was a name known in every Polish family. Children dreamed of becoming a patriot of his stature. Parents taking their babies to be christened chose the name Casimir in his honor.

But there was one person who found no joy in the actions of the Polish patriot. Empress Catherine, furious at the failures of her Russian soldiers, ordered up a new army to take on the Poles. Ten thousand Russian troops marched to Lithuania with orders to put down the Polish Confederates and capture Casimir Pulaski.

Learning of the planned attack, Casimir ordered his troops to hide in a giant Lithuania swamp. The Russians entered the murky area, only to be surrounded by Casimir's men. Again and again the Lithuanians struck the Russians, then hid carefully.

Casimir and Francis decided to return to Sambor for fresh troops and supplies. Taking a small company, Francis took the lead while Casimir brought up the rear. As Francis rode some distance ahead, he met two strangers. They told him that Casimir had been captured.

Quickly, Francis turned to ride back. Sadly, the two strangers were Russian soldiers in disguise, and Francis rode into a trap. Casimir spotted the enemy ahead and dispersed his men into the surrounding woods.

No Russian company of soldiers could ever capture Casimir Pulaski. Not when he did not wish to be found, that is. He stayed in the area, looking for Francis. But one night, a peasant family brought the young soldier sad news. They had seen a bloodstained uniform much like Casimir's own. Russian soldiers boasted that their general had hacked Francis Pulaski to death, then tried to sell his clothing. A weary guerilla colonel made plans to return to Sambor—alone.

No sooner had Casimir got on the road than a messenger brought more tragic news. Russian soldiers had attacked Winiary, burning it to the ground. Casimir asked about his mother and sisters. Had they escaped? The messenger could not tell him.

Casimir headed to Sambor, the sadness of his family's loss weighing heavily. He learned that Empress Catherine had offered a reward for his death. Anyone who helped him would be tortured to death.

While in Sambor, Casimir learned that the French leaders were finally going to send help. The Polish Confederates were gathering at Cracow where a French army would join them. A hopeful Casimir Pulaski left immediately for Cracow.

Soon after Casimir's arrival in Cracow, French general Charles-Francois Dumouriez arrived. But he brought only a few staff members. Where was his army? Dumouriez shook his head. An army wasn't necessary, he said. He could turn away the Russians with the Polish Confederates. By arming a string of fortresses, Dumouriez felt sure he could defend against any Russian attack. Casimir was shocked. Defend? What of guerilla attacks? The Polish soldiers were well trained in hit and run warfare. Dumouriez stood firm. Totally unimpressed with Casimir, he wrote home that Casimir was "a mere rascal" and "a bandit. I will have no use for his services. He knows nothing of military strategy."

Casimir ranted and raged. But his outbursts played into the French general's remarks about Casimir's youthfulness and rashness. The Polish Confederates supported Dumouriez. Disappointed, Casimir promised to follow the older leader's orders.

Dumouriez ordered Casimir to take a company of soldiers to Czestochowa, an old convent and fort. The place was a famous shrine of Poland, containing inside its heavy walls a painting of Mary, the mother of the Lord. Saint Luke was said to have painted the beloved picture, and Poles claimed it had helped save the country against aggressors. Although Casimir longed to face the enemy in a head-on encounter, he respected the importance of his assignment.

A new company of Russian soldiers, part of a major force raised to put down the Poles, arrived at Czestochowa before Casimir. They demanded that the people of the territory turn over all their jewels and valuables. Casimir and his troops arrived and broke up this threat. The young leader sent the Russians scurrying away.

Unfortunately, Casimir and his soldiers found no warm welcome inside Czestochowa. At first, the monks refused them entrance. Casimir begged entry as religious pilgrims on a peaceful mission. The monks agreed to let the visitors enter.

Once inside, Casimir knew there was much to be done to make Czestochowa safe. He welcomed Gen. Joseph Zaremba. A former leader of the Polish king's army, Zaremba was a close friend of the duchess of Courland. Feeling that the duchess had been poorly treated, Zaremba pledged to help her. She sent him to Casimir. Together, they made plans to defend Czestochowa. They hoped General Dumouriez would send soldiers, but instead he sent only a few staff officers.

Disappointed, yet not wanting to waste time, Casimir sprang into action. He ordered that the lead tiles on the roof be melted down into cannon balls. The tiles were replaced with clay and manure, which were fireproof. Soldiers carted in food from neighboring farms. Guns and muskets were repaired. Soldier stations were set up outside the fort to keep an eye on Russian troops in the area. General Zaremba was amazed at Casimir's quick action and military knowledge.

The second hungry "cat" had waited long enough on Poland's borders. For years Prussia had watched its neighbor closely, hopeful of pouncing and getting a share of the rich farmland and coast. Sure that the Russians would overcome the Polish uprising, the Prussians offered to send soldiers to help the Russians at Czestochowa. On January 1, 1771, Prussian cannon opened fire, blasting away at Czestochowa. "We shall control the fortress within a day," one Russian commander wrote home.

The Russian and Prussian soldiers were in for a big surprise. They had not anticipated the military skills of

Casimir Pulaski. He had molded Czestochowa into a defensive stronghold. The Polish soldiers inside shot only when their targets were sure. When enemy cannonballs bounced off the parapets, Casimir shouted, "God is on our side!" His cavalry, stationed outside the fortress walls, led charges against the back of enemy lines in the daytime. The Polish Confederates swooped in on the Russians and Prussians, catching them in a deadly cross fire. During the dark nighttime hours, Casimir led his troops in daring raids, cutting down surprised soldiers and tearing up cannon positions.

Russian leaders were furious and desperate. They rounded up area Polish peasants and marched them toward Czestochowa. Surely the Poles would not kill their own people. But Casimir had trained the Confederates well. They carefully picked off the enemy with precise sharpshooting.

Trying a new tactic, the Russians stormed the walls of Czestochowa. They leaned ladders against the walls and climbed up. But Casimir's soldiers were waiting. They pushed the ladders away and dropped stones down on the enemy. The Russians withdrew from the area, leaving almost two thousand dead soldiers to be buried.

Again, Casimir Pulaski was a hero. Poles praised his quick thinking and courage. Even the kings of other European nations sent their congratulations.

Casimir's victories angered Empress Catherine of Russia. "How can one man hold off our armies?" she demanded. Her leaders simply shook their heads.

But the cunning Catherine was not done yet. Slowly a plan took shape that she was sure would put an end to the triumphs of Casimir Pulaski.

Chapter Seven

Royal Kidnapping

The night breezes of Warsaw blew softly through the city streets. As King Stanislaus returned to the palace from a festive party, the wheels of the royal coach rattled over the ground. Parties helped the monarch forget the problems of the nation. Only hours before he had listened to the Russian ambassador make grim predictions. Repnin had warned that the Polish Confederates hoped to take over the country. According to Repnin, fighting the Russians and Prussians was merely a coverup of the Confederates to hide their true goal—to push out the king and claim Poland as their own.

The Polish king was puzzled. Why couldn't the Polish Confederates simply understand that the Russians wanted to keep the peace?

Unexpectedly, the coach jerked forward and quickened its pace. King Stanislaus peered out of the windows into the night. He heard the snap of reins and the shouts of his coachmen. Horsemen followed the coach in hot pursuit.

Suddenly a shot rang out. The driver reined the horses to a halt, his coachman companion slumped against him bleeding. Again King Stanislaus looked out into the night air, trying to identify the men who had halted his royal coach.

King Stanislaus could not believe what was happening. Who would dare stop the royal coach?

One of the horsemen moved his horse forward. He ordered King Stanislaus out of the coach and then gave him the reins to a riderless horse nearby.

Having little choice, King Stanislaus obeyed. Surrounded by his kidnappers, he was led out of town and into the countryside. On the group rode, in and out of villages and through dark woods. In one such patch, the kidnappers lost their way. Making matters worse, the king's horse stumbled and broke its leg.

It was daybreak by the time another horse arrived. In the sunlight King Stanislaus recognized a few of the men around him. They were part of the Polish Confederates. Seven years before they had pledged allegiance to their king. Now they had kidnapped him.

The monarch sensed the mood of the men. He asked them if he had ever harmed any one of them.

The kidnappers exchanged looks. Clearly these men were not cruel, hardened soldiers. They were merely soldiers sent to do a job. When King Stanislaus promised not to punish them if they returned him to the palace, the men agreed.

King Stanislaus was glad and grateful to return home. He spread the story of his capture, emphasizing his personal courage. As the tale traveled through Warsaw and beyond, it gathered colorful details. One version recounted how the king managed to slip away in the middle of the night and was chased for miles on horseback. He managed to escape the kidnappers by leaping over a giant gorge. When the king heard the story, he merely smiled silently.

Reaction to the story of the king's kidnapping was swift. Poles were outraged that their king had suffered through such an attack. Even people supporting the Polish Confederates were angry. From King Frederick of Prussia came an angry message. "A plot so horrible and atrocious covers the Confederates with shame. All the countries in Europe should unite to take vengeance on the crime."

Although Casimir Pulaski had played no part in the kidnapping, he was closely identified with the Confederates. Most people were sure he had to have known about the plot, even if he had not taken part in it.

King Stanislaus saw the chance to get rid of the threat of Casimir Pulaski once and for all. Although he did not accuse the Confederate leader personally, he did not deny his involvement whenever Pulaski's name was mentioned.

Talk of the king's kidnapping shocked Pulaski. He would never have taken part in such a plan. It was one thing to try to push foreign armies out of Poland. But to kidnap the king? Never! Stories reached Pulaski that not only was the king to have been kidnapped but he was supposed to have been killed. There were those who spoke of Pulaski as a "regicide," meaning a killer of a king.

Torn by the incident, Poles were confused and uncertain about their future. The Russians, Prussians, and Austrians took advantage of that confusion and went into action. They drew up maps, chopping Poland into territories among themselves. Then they plucked Polish generals out of the country and sent them to prisons in Siberia, Russia's coldest region. Polish armies were attacked and destroyed.

Too late the Poles realized that they had been tricked. Many suspected that spies of the devious Queen Catherine of Russia had infiltrated the ranks of the Polish Confederates and staged the king's kidnapping. Young Poles hurried to Czestochowa in hopes of helping Pulaski wage a strong battle against the foreign invaders.

Pulaski's first instinct was to fight, to the death if necessary. Yet, as a military leader, he knew the chances of winning were hopeless. He did not mind sacrificing his own life for his country, but the thought of losing thousands of other lives troubled him greatly. He wondered what to do. Then he made a decision.

In the early morning hours of June 1, 1772, Casimir

Pulaski donned the clothing of a peasant and slipped out the doors of the Czestochowa fortress. No one saw him leave. He left a note behind addressed to his top aides.

"I took up arms for the public good," Pulaski wrote. "For that same good I must lay them down. I do not want you to become linked with my misfortune. I know your courage, and know one day you will be able to display your zeal for your country again."

Pulaski's men wept openly. They knew he had not fled as a coward but as a hero. He could not bear to see all of them killed.

King Stanislaus rejoiced. Finally, he was rid of Pulaski. Little did the monarch realize that all he controlled was the city of Warsaw itself. Beyond that, the rest of Poland belonged to the hungry "cats" of Russia, Prussia, and Austria who divided the country into tasty morsels and munched contentedly.

Disguised and helped by Polish patriots, Pulaski slipped from place to place in Poland. In the summer of 1773, he was shocked to learn that he was being brought to trial on charges of kidnapping the king. Two other Polish Confederates were also being charged with the crime.

"Surely I will be found innocent of the charges," Pulaski wrote to a friend. "I would have no part in such a deed."

A stunned Casimir Pulaski learned that all those tried in the case had been found guilty. The punishment? Death by beheading. Then the bodies were to be displayed for public ridicule, burned, and the ashes thrown into the wind. As far as any possessions and land of Casimir Pulaski, they were to be turned over to the government.

Five years Pulaski had spent trying to free his beloved Poland from the hands of greedy neighbors. Now he had nothing. The label "traitor" hung around him like an invisible cloak. He was alone and confused. Where could he go? What could he do?

Chapter Eight

Into Prison

Pulaski stayed secretly with his longtime friend, the duke of Courland, for a few months. But the threat of discovery was too great. At Pulaski's request, the duke wrote to the king of France requesting safety for the Polish visitor in his country. No answer came.

Finally, Pulaski decided to head north into Prussia. Knowing there were those who might try to capture him, he took a new name—Rudzinski. But new name or not, the face and figure of Casimir Pulaski were well known. Learning he had been recognized by soldiers, the Polish leader fled in the night.

Discouraged and depressed, Pulaski roamed around Europe hoping for another opportunity to return to Poland safely. His face grew gaunt, his temper quick and fiery.

A chance to reclaim Poland from the Russian control appeared when the wealthy Prince Radziwil, a longtime Pulaski supporter, offered funds to build an army. But before Pulaski could pull forces together, Radziwil fell in love with a beautiful visitor to his court. Had the stranger been sent by Russia's empress Catherine? No one seemed to know, yet Prince Radziwil quickly withdrew his offer to help Pulaski and his men.

Disappointed but undaunted, Pulaski enlisted the help of a group of French officers who shared his desire to free Poland from Russia's hold. The sultan of Turkey was also

sympathetic to Pulaski's cause and offered his help. Turkey was fighting Russia too, and anything that would defeat the enemy was worth assisting.

But when the Russians sent the Turks fleeing, Pulaski knew his chances for additional support were dashed. He fled back to France with a few of his aides. At twenty-seven, Casimir Pulaski felt alone. Ten years before, the Poles had cheered his efforts as a courageous fighter for freedom. Now, he was without family or funds. To feed the five long-time friends who remained with him, he bought necessities on credit. But finally the bills came due—and overdue. French authorities arrested Pulaski and threw him in a debtors' prison in Marseilles.

Night and day Pulaski listened to the anguished cries of chained prisoners. The stench of human waste stung his nostrils. Most debtors stayed in cleaner chambers, and Pulaski's followers begged that he be moved. Still, he remained, week after week, in the filthiest part of the prison.

Pulaski's friends did not forget him. They wrote letters to Poland, telling the Confederates of his plight. Soon money rolled in to the Marseilles prison. Each contribution was put into the fund that would pay the debts of the former "guerilla colonel" and win his release. "This man should never be held prisoner," wrote one merchant in Warsaw. "He is a brave and noble hero."

Quickly the donations grew. In June of 1775, a gaunt and weary Casimir Pulaski stepped from the doorway of the Marseilles prison a free man. But now he faced new problems. Execution awaited him if he returned to Poland. The only life he knew was that of a soldier. But where does a soldier go without a war?

Chapter Nine
Big Decisions

On the other side of the world, a teapot was boiling. King George III of England was having a terrible time trying to get those "rebellious and ridiculous colonists" in America to take orders. They refused to pay the taxes imposed upon them, and they resented foreign troops on American soil.

There was little doubt where Pulaski's feelings lay. Whether Polish or British, kings seemed to be of the same nature. They sought to satisfy their own interests, often at the expense of their people. Pulaski read newspaper stories about the turmoil in America, and he also heard accounts of how King Stanislaus was dividing Poland into slices and giving them away to neighboring countries. Empress Catherine of Russia was getting her way. All the Polish Confederates were in exile, hoping someday to stage a revolution. But that day was far away, if ever to come, and no one knew that better than Casimir Pulaski. He would never be allowed back in his beloved country.

Each day Pulaski walked along the docks of the Marseilles harbor. Men loaded ships with cannon and ammunition, ships headed for the American colonies. Spanish flags, a safe protection against British interception, snapped high on the masts. Longtime rivals of the powerful British navy, the Spanish Armada supported the American colonists. The urge to join the colonial cause for freedom grew inside Pulaski. Finally, he made a decision. He would go to America.

However, it was not that easy. There were many adventurers who wished to head to the colonies and fight in the revolution against the British. Pulaski wrote to the count de Rhuliere, an old family friend who was living in Paris. He was a member of the French Academy and knew many government officials, especially in the Ministry of Foreign Affairs. It was the count who had helped Pulaski when he came to France, even giving the Pole in hiding an assumed name. Perhaps the kind friend would provide one more favor.

The count de Rhuliere considered Pulaski's plea. He took the young Pole's petition to the American ambassador Benjamin Franklin. At seventy, Franklin enjoyed a reputation as being a wise and kind statesman. The ambassador studied Pulaski's request, then sent word that he could go to America. However, there were two major conditions. First, he must travel secretly, not telling anyone in France or Poland where he was headed. After all, many others wished to go also—and King Stanislaus would not approve of the Americans helping a Polish fugitive. Secondly, Pulaski could have free passage from Brittany to America if he went alone. Pulaski had hoped to take a few of his loyal followers, but that request was denied. Franklin wanted to meet Pulaski personally and invited him to Paris.

It was a nervous Casimir Pulaski who entered the small but elegant house of Ambassador Franklin in the Passy district of Paris. The Pole had once owned fine jackets, laced shirts, clean buckled shoes. Now, his attire was dingy and drab, a sad contrast to the bygone days of the Winiary.

But Benjamin Franklin cared little what his guest wore. He was more interested in how he felt about fighting for the colonial cause. By the end of their visit, Franklin hurried Pulaski on his way. The American ambassador was convinced the young Pole would be a big help to General Washington.

As he prepared to travel across the sea, Pulaski received surprising news. His sister Anna wrote that his name had been cleared. If he wanted, he could return to Poland and live quietly. Not only that, she sent fifteen thousand livres as a share of the Pulaski family funds.

What to do? Casimir Pulaski faced a big decision.

Chapter Ten

Ahoy, America!

Casimir Pulaski knew that if he left Europe, he would never return to his beloved Poland. Yet it would never be the country he knew and loved. The hungry "cat" Russia had captured the proud "mouse" it had sought for so many years. Empress Catherine smiled from her Russian throne, while King Stanislaus seemed satisfied at filling his castle with priceless paintings and listening to visiting musicians perform at grand state banquets. Yes, Pulaski would be able to return to Poland if he promised to be quiet and uninvolved. Quiet and uninvolved? That was hardly Casimir Pulaski's nature. With energy and enthusiasm, he packed his bag—a very small bag—and prepared to head for America.

In May of 1777, Casimir Pulaski boarded the SS *Reprisal* as it sat in the harbor of Nantes, France. On the surface, the vessel appeared to be a trading clipper ship, but the ruggedly built craft housed ammunition and supplies destined for the American colonists. The contents of the boat were top secret, or supposed to be. But British spies knew the truth. There was no secret about the *Reprisal*'s most notorious passenger either. "The Americans have hired that assassin Pulaski," the British ambassador wrote his government colleagues in London.

Leaders of the British navy quickly dispatched two of their star frigates loaded with cannon to the English Channel. Their orders? To blow the *Reprisal* out of the water. The

British leaders had no intention of allowing a shipload of
enemy supplies and ammunition to reach the American
colonists. And the prospect of a thirty-year-old Polish military hero helping the revolutionaries did not please the
British either. British officials were convinced that the
Reprisal had to be sunk.

But nature took the colonial side. A head wind caught
the *Reprisal* in its grip and threw it off its course. The
British frigates waited without result as their target slipped
safely into the Atlantic and headed toward America.

Pulaski found a new world aboard the *Reprisal*. The
Pole had never heard English spoken, and the salty, tough
language of the sailors offered a fresh excitement. The
entire workings of the vessel delighted Pulaski. He climbed
to the top of the crow's nest, gazing across the endless
waters as far as he could see. He journeyed into the bowels
of the ship as well, asking crew members questions as to
how the craft was built, its strengths and weaknesses.
Ropes fascinated him, and he climbed among the riggings
like a human spider. When he was not exploring the ship,
he learned to make knots.

The sight of another ship in the distance brought the
Reprisal crew to battle stations. Pulaski stood ready to
assist a cannon crew if the approaching craft sported an
enemy flag. The sailors braced themselves for combat. But
when the other ship posted an American flag, a collective
sigh ran through the *Reprisal* crew. Ready as they were for
action, they much preferred a trip without skirmish.

That's exactly what they got. The *Reprisal* sailed
smoothly through the waters of the Atlantic. Borrowing the
captain's books about navigation, Pulaski became an eager
student, studying how soldiers might be transported by sea
to help soldiers moving on land. Enemy troops could be
caught in the middle and defeated. Perhaps there might
even be an entire branch of the military trained to serve
aboard ships.

Each night Pulaski read over the letter of introduction written by the American ambassador Benjamin Franklin. Hopefully, George Washington would have a specific job that needed to be done. Casimir Pulaski did not want to be just another soldier. He wanted to make a difference. Carefully, by candlelight, Pulaski laid out battle plans and strategy. He did not know the geography of the American colonies, but there were certain military maneuvers suitable for most situations.

So often ocean-going vessels fought angry storms, the helpless wooden crafts being tossed and rolled in the waves. But once again, nature smiled on the SS *Reprisal,* guiding it smoothly through the water under sunny skies.

"Land ho!"

The shout from the lookout in the crow's nest brought a joyful echo of cheers from the ship's crew. Although the trip had been pleasantly uneventful, a month aboard the vessel was enough for the sailors. No one was happier to drop anchor in Massachusetts' Marblehead Bay on July 23, 1777, than Casimir Pulaski. He had spent his time well aboard the ship, but he was eager to meet General Washington and offer his services.

Casimir Pulaski had spent half of his thirty years as a soldier. He was experienced and well trained compared to most of the American colonial soldiers. Despite the hot July weather, Pulaski donned his heavy wool military outfit and reported to Gen. Ambrose Heath who commanded the American forces in Boston. Fortunately, Heath spoke French and communicated easily with the recently arrived Pole. For hours they hovered over tables, carefully studying the battles on paper. Heath soon realized the skill and quick thinking of his new friend. As for Pulaski, he could see that he had arrived at an important moment. The months ahead could spell victory or defeat for the colonial army.

Hoping to keep his visitor in Boston, Heath took Pulaski

on a complete review of the fortifications around the city. Pulaski was impressed. There was no doubt that Boston was well protected. But it was largely that fact that encouraged Pulaski to leave. The British were not about to attack the colonial forces at Boston. Such action would meet quick defeat. Pulaski wanted to join the fighting forces in the field. He was used to commanding troops engaged in active combat. Hopefully, he would get such a chance.

The trip from Boston to Philadelphia, the colonial capital where General Washington had his headquarters, was a long journey by horseback. Heath tried to discourage his Polish visitor from making it. Yet Pulaski was used to riding, and he was determined to meet the colonial commander. With carefully drawn maps and directions, Pulaski rode away from Boston on a horse given to him by Heath.

Surely, having a horse beneath him felt good to Pulaski. The long voyage across the sea had offered little chance to enjoy the thrill of riding a sure-footed animal. The sights of the New England countryside were not unlike those in Poland—handsome fields, neat and sturdy farmhouses, quaint villages and inns. He was happy to find a ferry across the Hudson River near Beacon, New York, then headed across the New Jersey plains burning away under a scorching August sun. Another ferry carried Pulaski and his horse across the Delaware River at Trenton. He rode toward Philadelphia, eager to meet General Washington who was headquartered on Neshanning Creek, a few miles south of the city.

Once in the camp, Pulaski had barely dismounted when he was greeted by another European, a handsome twenty-year-old Frenchman. The marquis de Lafayette had also been attracted to embrace the American cause and had traveled across the sea to offer his services. Among the letters Pulaski brought from France was one from the marquise de Lafayette to her husband. It was the first letter the young nobleman had received from his wife, and he broke the seal eagerly and read it at once. Having finished, he offered to take Pulaski to General Washington and to serve as interpreter between the two military heros.

It was a cheerful meeting. Pulaski's delight at meeting the man he had traveled so far to see, and General Washington's clear interest in the man who had been so highly touted by Ambassador Franklin. As interpreter, Lafayette had his work cut out for him. Both men spoke freely with much warm and mutual regard. However, when Pulaski asked for a commission to serve as a general in the colonial army, General Washington begged off. The commander-in-chief of the American army could not grant such a request. Only the Continental Congress could approve such an assignment.

Pulaski could not hide his frustration and disappointment. His light skin reddened as he beat one fist into the open palm of his other hand. However, he left Washington's headquarters determined to get the commission he wanted.

Both Washington and Lafayette wrote letters praising the background and credentials of Pulaski. But the impatient Pole wanted to make his wishes even stronger, to enhance his chances even more. He wrote a letter too, but his English was so bad the Congressional Commission in Philadelphia thought Pulaski wanted to take Washington's place as commander-in-chief. The commission sent the Polish patriot back to Washington. "Please advise us clearly as to your intentions regarding this gentleman," the commission requested of the general.

Washington did not waste a moment. The colonial commander asked that Congress immediately appoint Pulaski as head of the American cavalry. Noting that Poland had long used soldiers on horseback as part of their military strength, Washington pointed out that Pulaski had both skill and experience leading cavalry riders. Not only that, he had the spirit to fight. "This gentleman, like us," wrote Washington, "has been engaged in defending the liberty and independence of his country and has sacrificed his fortune in his zeal for these objects."

Pulaski carried Washington's request to the commission in Philadelphia, then returned to the Neshanning Creek headquarters to await an answer. He had little doubt that action would be swift. After all, Lafayette had never had a day of military experience and the Continental Congress had quickly made the twenty-year-old Frenchman an honorary major general at Washington's request. Surely the congress would act at once in behalf of a trained and experienced military leader like Pulaski.

But the hours slipped into days with no word from Philadelphia. News did arrive that Lord William Howe and his British troops had landed on the shores of Chesapeake Bay on August 31, 1777, and that they were already marching the sixty miles toward Philadelphia. Pulaski jumped on his horse and rode to the city. Learning that no action had been taken on his request, he angrily hurried back to Washington's headquarters. If he could not be granted a commission as a general, he would fight as a common soldier.

Washington would not hear of such a thing. He immediately appointed Pulaski as one of his aides. That way, the Polish fighter could be close to the action and lend his ideas.

As Howe's troops advanced toward Philadelphia, Washington knew there was little he could do to save the city from enemy hands. The American troops he commanded were in sad condition. Typhus, dysentery, and smallpox took far more lives than battle combats. Adequate medical care was not available.

Often, groups of the state militias were called home at crucial times of fighting. This angered Casimir Pulaski who was eager to build a strong cavalry. In Poland, those men fighting for the Knights of the Holy Cross stood united in battle. In order to boost morale and worry the enemy, Washington spread stories that the Continental Army boasted many more soldiers than was true.

Once, when an American officer requested permission to arrest a British spy, Washington shook his head. "Don't arrest him," said the colonial commander-in-chief. "Invite him to dinner and then, as if by accident, drop a hint that the army has twelve thousand men."

Quickly, Pulaski sized up the American situation. As well as being outnumbered, the colonial soldiers were inexperienced, undertrained, and undisciplined. They carried an assorted collection of firearms and wore their own clothing of woodsmen and farmers. With these men, Washington decided to take a stand against Howe's soldiers at Chadds Ford on Brandywine Creek on September 11, 1777.

It was a frustrated Casimir Pulaski who followed General Washington around as they studied the possible areas for engaging the enemy. Maps were inadequate, leaving out various woods and creeks. Before new documents could be made, the British troops approached. Again, Washington received faulty information, underestimating the size of the British troops and misreading their positions. The Americans focused on the enemy soldiers moving forward in the open. Meanwhile, Lord Charles Cornwallis and his troops were sweeping around the American soldiers in hopes of encircling them. Scouting the forthcoming conflict, Pulaski spotted the British plan and alerted the closest general, John Sullivan. He relayed the message to Washington, who had little time to react. The British hit the Americans head-on. The colonists fought bravely, but Washington was forced to order his men into retreat. They backstepped to Chester with their supplies, allowing Howe to take over Philadelphia.

Pulaski begged Washington to give him a small group of cavalrymen, thirty would be enough. If the Americans had to retreat, it should be done with care and life-saving efficiency. The right wing of the colonial army was ready to fall apart, and Pulaski was sure he could pull it back together. Washington agreed to give his new aide a chance.

Seated atop his horse in front of his men, Pulaski faced

a major obstacle even before reaching the British troops. He knew his small company did not understand Polish. But if they could not understand his language, they would understand his actions. Waving a saber wildly above his head and pulling the reins of his horse so that the beast reared high into the air, Pulaski charged ahead. His men followed, imitating their leader's every move.

The British were caught off guard. Who was this shouting madman? Who were these wild, yelling men who came waving swords and brandishing flintlock pistols? The American soldiers on foot were also startled. With the sight and sounds of the cavalry riding forward, many of the colonists found new spirit and forced the British infantry back.

Despite Pulaski's contributions, the Battle of Brandywine was a major defeat for the Americans. But Pulaski's quick actions provided a safer retreat for Washington's soldiers and saved many lives. The Polish hero was now an American hero. He had proved that he had the power to rouse men to do his bidding, and that soldiers on horseback could be a valuable addition to America's military fighting strength.

The Continental Congress made a quick exit out of Philadelphia before Lord Howe's troops arrived on September 27, 1777. But Pulaski received the commission he had requested. Washington wasted no time in naming the new brigadier general Pulaski chief of cavalry. Undoubtedly, he was eager to show how important soldiers on horseback could be to a military campaign.

But a long, grim winter lay ahead.

Chapter Eleven
Cavalry Chief

Now that he was in a position to command, Casimir Pulaski probably wished to shout "Give me a chance!" He wanted to organize men, drill them in riding and shooting, perfect their every skill as soldiers on horseback. Pulaski could not remember his life without riding. So much could be done on horseback that could not be accomplished on foot. There was so much opportunity for mobility, of swift movement, either by the individual soldier or as a group.

But other American generals did not understand this principle. They had worked little with soldiers on horseback. They thought of such men only as scouts. Each day the generals asked for men to keep watch around their troops. Pulaski's assigned cavalry was always divided, constantly roaming the countryside in search of the enemy. Pulaski's efforts to train a special group of fighting men were thwarted.

Washington's troops slowly retreated. Each day Pulaski led his men on horseback, and roamed the area fields and hillsides, making sure no British soldiers crept too close.

Early one morning, Pulaski and his cavalry stumbled upon a huge regiment of enemy troops moving swiftly forward. Several of the brigadier general's cavalry wanted to flee, to rejoin Washington and the main army. But Pulaski would not hear of such a thing. With a drawn sword, he ordered his men to fan out in a line. It was the old standard

military move of making the enemy think you have more soldiers than you do. Then he led them forward, directly into the approaching soldiers. Taken by surprise, the British thought it was the entire American army attacking. The enemy redcoats retreated, and Pulaski hastily galloped back to Washington to report the news. When guards tried to prevent Pulaski from interrupting a meeting, the cavalry chief pushed his way through. In broken English, he explained what he had seen.

Colonel Alexander Hamilton shook his head. He was convinced that Pulaski was confused, that the Pole had probably seen an American regiment.

Pulaski was outraged. He might not be able to speak English well, but he knew what he had seen. After all, he had just led his cavalrymen into a head-on attack.

Washington sided with his cavalry chief. The colonial commander ordered three hundred foot soldiers to join the horse soldiers. He also ordered Gen. Charles Scott of his staff to assist Pulaski. It was essential the advancing British troops be stopped.

For the first time since his arrival, Pulaski truly felt like a general. He shouted orders as clearly as he could, lining up men behind stone walls. General Scott's men moved into position behind stone walls and trees. As the British soldiers advanced, the Americans opened fire.

The redcoats stopped their march, sprinting in every direction for safety. Many fell back, retreating from the shower of musket balls.

Pulaski scampered across the lines of skirmish, calling out encouragement to the men. What a triumph this could be! Ordered to merely block the British advance, they had the enemy retreating. Perhaps this could be an American victory!

K-boom! A clap of thunder shook the hillside, followed by rain in sheets pounding the countryside. It poured down, soaking the musket gunpowder so that men could not fire their weapons. Schuylkill Creek quickly became an angry snake of water, threatening to cut off Pulaski and his men from Washington's troops. The cavalry chief ordered his men to back off. The British troops were in retreat anyway, and the mission had been accomplished.

Hour after hour the rain continued, water and mud rising to the knees of horses and soldiers alike. No campfires could be lit, no muskets fired. The Americans trudged slowly through the thick murk, trying to gain rest standing up against trees or sprawling on soaked branches. The British, seeking sleep under ceilings, took refuge in Germantown.

Gathering his officers, Washington plotted an attack against the British at Germantown. He planned to converge his men by four roads into the town in a surprise raid at dawn.

The plan took form. Slowly, cautiously, the Americans crept toward Germantown early on the morning of October 4, 1777. Men moved silently, their steps muffled in the soaked ground while the cavalry rode horses, their hooves wrapped in cloth to deaden their sounds. When all was in position, Casimir Pulaski galloped forward, leading his men on horseback.

Guards at the British outposts were caught totally off guard. They left their positions, scurrying back to their main forces.

Then, once again, nature turned against the Americans. The skies opened, hosing the entire area with thick rain. Fog draped the area like heavy smoke. Soldiers could see only a few feet in front of them. Colonists found themselves shooting each other by mistake. In all the confusion, Lord Cornwallis ordered two battalions of his men out of Philadelphia, and they helped drive the Americans off. A sad Washington counted some 1071 soldiers lost, although some British cannons were captured.

Pulaski admired Washington personally. Yet the Polish

leader felt the American commander was not making the best use of his army. There was so much more the soldiers on horseback could do, especially armed with lances. After the Germantown fracas, Pulaski had a lance made and sent it by special messenger to Congress. He proposed the entire cavalry be given lances. Some members of Congress were shocked at Pulaski's suggestion. After all, who was this foreigner who was suddenly trying to tell them how to win a war? How successful had he been in his home country of Poland? And what was so special about a cavalry? A soldier on foot was just as brave as a soldier on horseback. Maybe more so. No, there would be no lances, the Congress decided.

Pulaski was not the only general rebuffed by the Congress. During the winter of 1777-78, General Washington was criticized again and again. Some openly recommended his removal, with Gen. Horatio Gates being put in his place. Pulaski was close enough to know why. Gates was not only a good general, he was an able politician. He constantly sugarcoated his military reports, downplaying his losses and trumpeting his victories. Washington was more open and honest with Congress, and they did not like hearing complaints about unpaid salaries, lack of uniforms, and insufficient weapons.

Pulaski swallowed his anger at being rebuked by Congress and pledged to help Washington all he could. He trained a small group of cavalrymen and waged surprise raids whenever they came upon British soldiers. At the Battle of Chestnut Hill, the American foot soldiers were fleeing when Pulaski arrived on the scene. Waving his sword high, the Polish general raced forward. His men followed on his horse's heels. The colonial troops regained their lost spirit and turned around. They sent the redcoats running. Defeat was turned into victory.

Pulaski longed for a true cavalry corps. He was convinced he could train men quickly, then get them into the action to help the infantry. He wrote to Washington, "When we are superior in cavalry, the enemy will not dare to extend theirs. We will then have many opportunities of attacking and destroying him by degrees. But if they have it in their power to augment their cavalry, they can do the same to us and ours will suffer and dwindle away. Our army dispersed and pursued by horsemen will be unable to rally. Our baggage can be captured, our officers taken, our losses fatal."

Pulaski's arguments were strong. Unfortunately, his timing was bad. Washington was in no position to demand anything more from Congress. Too many members grumbled about the colonial losses at Brandywine and Germantown. The name "Horatio Gates" kept coming up as a successor to Washington.

How well Pulaski remembered the winters in Poland, when the Knights of the Holy Cross engaged the Russian soldiers of Empress Catherine. The soldiers on horseback had won many battles against the enemy, the surefootedness and speed of the cavalry steeds proving deciding factors against the enemy. If only . . .

But Washington would not permit Pulaski to build up and train more cavalry soldiers. The other generals were unconvinced of such a need. The soldiers on horseback were needed to patrol and to scout. But the thought of a separate cavalry corps traveled no further than Valley Forge, where the bulk of the colonial army lay headquartered during that long winter of 1777-78. Recognizing that the horses could not endure the cold and snow there, Pulaski requested they be moved to Trenton. Finally, he got a wish granted.

Having his suggestions be ignored was only one disappointment to Pulaski. Again and again he came upon men making fun of his poor English. Even his sword-raising tactics, so often successful in rallying the American troops, were imitated and laughed at. One officer, Col. Stephen Moylan, was especially brutal. He went so far as to grow a trim moustache like Pulaski's, to make his performance more amusing.

Pulaski welcomed his Polish cousin John Zelinski in January of 1778. The former Knight of the Holy Cross came to Trenton when he learned of his relative's appointment as head of the cavalry. Zelinski was not made so welcome by Colonel Moylan, who now had another Pole whose speech he could make fun of among the troops.

When Pulaski and Zelinski, a newly appointed lieutenant, encountered Moylan during a scouting tour one afternoon, a shouting match began. Moylan threw out one insult too many, and Pulaski demanded an apology. Moylan refused, and in a flurry of action, Moylan ended up knocking Zelinski to the ground.

Pulaski was furious. He ordered Moylan arrested and brought up on a court martial charge. Unfortunately, several officers hearing the case resented the Polish foreigners trying to rid the colonial army of "a full blooded American soldier." Moylan was freed. Pulaski protested the court's action to Washington, but the commander simply backed up the action of the court's officials. Zelinski was outraged. Claiming Moylan had insulted his honor, the Pole challenged the American officer to a duel. "I'll not duel a bloody foreigner," Moylan declared, "but I'll sure horsewhip him."

The next time the two men met they were both on horseback. Colonel Moylan drew his sword, while Zelinski pulled out a short lance hanging from his saddle. Using skill and speed, the Polish cavalryman swatted the American's horse who neatly deposited him on the ground. A laughing Zelinski rode off, leaving a shouting Moylan chasing his steed.

Moylan and other unfriendly officers were not the only problems faced that long winter of 1777-78. Food and provisions ran short. New England farmers and merchants preferred to sell to the British because they could pay more. No one was sure the Continental dollars printed by the Americans would have value.

Pulaski had little use for those people supporting the enemy. He commandeered both horses and provisions, offering to pay in Continental money. If it was refused, Pulaski took what he needed and paid nothing. This was war, after all, not business. The merchants and farmers, especially the Quakers who opposed war on religious grounds, complained to Congress. Soon Washington sent orders to Pulaski to stop his tactics.

It was difficult for Pulaski to understand the American ways of fighting a war. Certainly there had been disagreements among the generals when he fought in Poland. But the bickering seldom intruded upon the goal of liberty and freedom. Since entering the colonial fighting, it seemed there were as many fights among the military leadership as there were against the enemy. Congress, too, seemed much like the enemy at times. It seemed unwilling to help provide food, weapons, ammunition, and other necessities.

Whenever he could, Pulaski tried to set up drills for his cavalrymen. Yet the requests continued to come in, pulling his soldiers on horseback away from any unified maneuvers. Although he was supposed to be responsible to General Washington, other generals tried to give him orders and use his men. When Gen. Anthony Wayne called upon Pulaski to help him, the Pole agreed. After all, he would not ignore the call of a comrade in battle.

Once Pulaski and Wayne teamed up, they were a force to be reckoned with. They argued constantly about methods and times for attack, playing cat and mouse with British colonel Thomas Stirling along the Delaware River. Wayne came to appreciate the power of soldiers on horseback. He, himself, understood the importance of leading a charge into enemy troops so that his own men would follow. Neither cared much about personal glory. American freedom from England was the cause of this war, and until that was won, little else mattered.

Once, having driven Stirling's troops to the shore of the

Delaware, Pulaski and Wayne put together a brilliant plan. Pulaski's cavalry stood wedged between Wayne's foot soldiers. As Pulaski charged directly into the enemy lines, Wayne's soldiers slowly moved forward, squeezing closer all the time. Desperately Stirling signaled for help from British ships in the Delaware. Cannonball after cannonball exploded in the midst of the colonial regiments, forcing them to retreat.

Pulaski continued his brave rides among his men, shouting encouragement and pushing them ahead. Suddenly, his horse went down, tossing the surprised Pole to the ground. Three men raced to their leader's side, fearing the worst.

"I need another horse!" Pulaski yelled, his legs a bit shaky as he struggled to his feet. "Bring me another horse."

In minutes he was back in the midst of the fighting. Such action instilled his men with fresh energy and courage. Forward they galloped and ran, shouting with the same force as their leader. The encounter was declared an American victory, and stories of Pulaski's personal bravery passed quickly around the campfires of the colonial soldiers.

Wayne, also, praised Pulaski. In writing his report, Wayne noted that his partner "behaved with his usual courage and bravery and put his cavalry to good use. Without him this victory would not have been possible."

But Pulaski remained disgruntled. How much he wanted to build his soldiers on horseback into a major offensive weapon, a disciplined cavalry capable of attacking the enemy and scoring victories. Yet no one seemed able to recognize the cavalry's potential. It was merely a help to the true Continental army. When the infantry needed assistance, call in the cavalry.

On March 14, 1778, Casimir Pulaski resigned his commission as a brigadier general. But he gave Washington more than his resignation. He drew up a plan for a special legion of both cavalry and infantry soldiers. Independent of other military branches, this mobile unit would act only under Washington's direction. It would be no part of the four cavalry regiments that were always being used as scouting brigades by other generals. In Pulaski's thoughts was a well-trained and disciplined military unit capable of quick, precisioned action. It was an understanding Washington who accepted Pulaski's resignation, and a wise Washington who supported Pulaski's plan for a new legion. Not only did Congress support Pulaski's plan, they also gave him fifty thousand dollars to hire and outfit new members of his legion. Considering the short supply of money that existed, it was clear the members of Congress had gained new respect for the patriot from Poland.

Casimir Pulaski knew that much was expected of him. He hoped and prayed he could live up to those expectations.

Chapter Twelve

Building a Legion

Pulaski did not waste a minute. The winter of 1777-78 had been hard on the Continental army, particularly those who had suffered from the intense cold and snow at Valley Forge, Pennsylvania. The Americans needed renewed spirit and action, preferably in the form of military victories. Pulaski decided to set up his own legion headquarters in Baltimore, Maryland. He carefully put together a training program for soldiers on horseback.

Congress had set the number for the new legion. Pulaski was authorized sixty-eight horsemen and two hundred foot soldiers. Washington told Pulaski to pick a few officers from each of the existing cavalry regiments. Many of these men were foreigners, having traveled across the sea as Pulaski had done. Among those the new legion commander picked were his cousin, Lt. John Zelinski, and a Frenchman, Paul Bentalou, a longtime friend of Pulaski.

To get recruits for his new legion, Pulaski dispersed his top officers to Maryland, New Jersey, Pennsylvania, and Virginia. Soon an announcement appeared in colonial newspapers:

All who desire to distinguish themselves in the service of their country are invited to enlist in the Legion. Opportunity will be offered to enterprising, brave, vigilant soldiers. They will prefer the Legion to other services not

destined to harass the enemy so much. As time for action is approaching, those desiring to distinguish themselves should apply immediately.

Pulaski's frustration from the past showed through. His legion would make a difference. There was no doubt in his mind.

The new legion commander was also sure how to outfit his men. From saddlemaker to saddlemaker he galloped, inspecting their wares. He demanded the best, nothing fancy, but a saddle that would hold together and last, with sturdy saddlebags. Lances were required, made of wood that would bend without snapping, and with iron tips. Then there were the carbines and cartridge boxes. Pulaski wanted his legion to be well armed.

Not only that, the proud Polish leader wanted his men well uniformed too. He selected shirts and socks, even underdrawers the lancers would wear. Handsome caps and sky blue cloaks were carefully selected, with wool linings in a variety of colors including scarlet, white, yellow, and green. Why? So Pulaski could break the men into separate companies, and he could tell instantly from which company each legionnaire hailed.

To set his legion off even more, Pulaski ordered ten thousand gold metal buttons for uniform trim. "I feel like a general myself in this fancy outfit," one soldier wrote to his family back home.

Pulaski wanted his men to feel special. After all, he hoped his legion of lancers would carry out military missions no one else could.

But it was not outer appearances that would make a quality cavalry. It was training, discipline, and self-pride. Pulaski set up an exhausting schedule for his recruits. By early summer of 1778, Pulaski's men rolled out of bed at sunup and spent the day on horseback. In one hand each man carried a sword, in the other hand, a lance. Across fields they galloped, slashing at stuffed dummies tied against posts and trees. The men filled the air with loud shouts, cheering each other's actions. Sweat soaked deeply into clothing, the afternoon sun broiling the men as they drilled. Yet Pulaski canceled no training exercises because of the heat. "Battles are fought in fair weather and foul," he told his troops.

Recruits flocked to join Pulaski's legion, attracted by stories of the Pole's heroism in past battles. Funds promised from Congress trickled in. In need of more money for uniforms and supplies, Pulaski wrote his sister Anna in Poland. From her convent, the nun sent sixteen thousand dollars from the sale of family lands. Pulaski immediately spent the money for supplies.

After many weeks of drill, Pulaski put his cavalry on display for the people of Baltimore. The August 4, 1778, issue of the *Maryland Journal* reports:

> General Pulaski reviewed his independent legion in this town. Their martial appearance excited the admiration of all. They performed many maneuvers in a manner that reflected the highest honor on both officers and privates.

Pulaski was proud of his men. But it was one thing to parade before friendly citizens and another to successfully attack the enemy. Impatiently, Pulaski awaited orders for military service.

Days drifted into weeks and no word came from Congress or Washington. Pulaski kept drilling his men, but they, too, grew weary with waiting. Since the Continental army had managed to drive the British out of Philadelphia, the American Congress was again meeting in the capital city. Pulaski decided to parade his troops right in front of the Congressmen's noses. Then, perhaps, they would order the legion into action.

Under a blazing September sun, Pulaski's legionnaires

strutted before government officials and Philadelphians. At the front of their parade they carried a red satin banner which the Moravian sisters at Bethlehem, Pennsylvania, had beautifully embroidered. On one side of the banner was a picture of the all-seeing Eye of God. Thirteen stars, representing the thirteen colonies, surrounded the eye and the Latin words *Non Alius Regit* (None Other Rules) appeared nearby. On the other side of the banner, "U.S." was circled with the words *Unita Virtus Fortier* (Union Makes for Valor).

Pulaski led his legion forward to the enthusiastic cheers of the people assembled. Each legionnaire, nodding graciously to the bystanders, sat proudly mounted on his horse. The sky blue cloaks on the soldiers were tossed back on one shoulder to reveal the colors of each division. The golden buttons sparkled like new coins in the afternoon sun. To the sound of bugles and drums, the legionnaires marched. Surely there was no one more proud that day than a thirty-one-year-old patriot from Poland.

Chapter Thirteen

A Taste of Victory

Quickly Casimir Pulaski broke open the seal to the document he held. It was a communication from General Washington. "As soon as the Board gives the Legion the order to move, they are to join my Army east of New York City, at Kingsbridge on the North River. If, as you pass through Jersey, the enemy has landed in that state, give General Maxwell every assistance you can with your troops." Finally, the official orders had arrived. The date was September 19, 1778.

Early the next morning Pulaski's legion marched out of the city of Philadelphia. This time there were no crowds, no drums and bugles, no cheers. Only the clatter of horses' hooves and the creaking of wagon wheels on cobblestone streets broke the stillness of the early morning hours. As the slender ribbon of men moved along the road toward Trenton, a messenger rode up with another communication from General Washington. Pulaski's cavalry corps was to proceed to Barnegat Bay off the Jersey shore. British troops at Egg Harbor were tearing up the area, raiding stores and warehouses. Not only that, the American colonial vessels had been successfully skirting the blockade at the mouth of the Delaware River. No doubt the British hoped to stop that at once!

The Pulaski troops wasted no time. Eager for action, they headed straight toward Egg Harbor. By the time they arrived on October 6, once-proud study buildings stood like burned-out shells. The villages of Chestnut Hills and Bay's River Neck huddled under giant clouds of deep smoke. The sounds of rampaging British soldiers echoed across the countryside.

Sizing up the situation, Pulaski threw his men into action. He sent one company of his cavalrymen to block the British from land retreat. Another company was sent to the beaches so the British could not escape by ship.

"But what if they will not surrender?" one legionnaire wondered.

A somber Pulaski shook his head. Every effort would be made to allow the enemy soldiers to lay down their weapons and give up. If they refused, they would be cut down. Such were the rules of war.

Pulaski's men dispersed to their respected areas. In the next hours, the British soldiers ran for safety. But most were captured. Those who would not surrender felt the fatal swing of the legionnaires' swords.

News of Pulaski's victory at Egg Harbor traveled quickly among the colonial camps. General Washington was overjoyed. It was not merely the number of casualties or captives that was important; it was momentum. The Continental army had to feel it was winning the war. Soldiers who are winning fight with greater determination. They do not complain as much, and they are willing to make sacrifices. So often it seemed Casimir Pulaski's actions brought about colonial victories. The fact that he was a foreigner impressed the American soldiers even more. After all, he had no family to protect in this country, no home or business to go back to. He was fighting for freedom, nothing more, nothing less.

No sooner had Pulaski transferred his British prisoners and finished up other military business around Egg Harbor, new orders arrived from General Washington. The British quartered in Fort Niagara near Minisink, New

York, were raiding area settlements. Indians were helping them. An American fort nearby needed strengthening. General Washington ordered Pulaski's cavalry there.

The American wilderness was new territory to Pulaski and to his other officers. Yet his experiences as a soldier in the Polish mountains came in handy as the colonial legionnaires traveled the high, rugged mountain routes along the Delaware River. Slowly and cautiously the wagons creaked along the pathways. Often the moving column of men and horses stopped to clear rubble from the road. It was frustrating for the Polish patriot who always wanted to move swiftly. But there was no choice.

After the mountains came the forests, thick matted woodlands of trees and brush. The trails were jagged, causing the horses' feet to become bloodied and blistered. New horseshoes were needed often, and forges had to be set up for the traveling blacksmiths to work.

When the legion arrived at Cole's Fort, they received a big surprise. It was gone—burned to the ground. The bodies of its defenders had been mutilated. The thought of American soldiers being scalped by British Tories or Indians raised the tempers of Pulaski's men. They turned their anger to energy as they chopped down trees to build a new fort. Disgusted and disgruntled, Pulaski sent Congress a quick note dated November 26, 1778. "I desired to be employed near the enemy's line," the cavalry chief wrote. "I find myself placed in a wilderness where there are only bears to fight."

Bears were not the only obstacle nature threw at the Pulaski legion. Food was another. Few provisions remained from what the soldiers had brought, and area barns were bare. Pulaski fired off a letter to General Washington requesting cannon for the new fort and permission to send his cavalry where more food was available.

General Washington sent word that the infantry would remain in Minisink and the cavalry would locate in Easton,

Pennsylvania. The division kept Pulaski busy riding between the locations as well as making extra trips to appear before Congress in Philadelphia. Money was running low, and officials expected a close accounting of all bills and expenditures.

Within a few weeks, food in Easton ran out for the horses. Washington's decision to move the horses farther south troubled Pulaski. His foot soldiers and cavalry would be more separated. What kind of war was this? His men grew bored with inactivity. The awareness that an American infantry lay camped in Minisink undoubtedly kept away British attacks. But that thought offered Pulaski little satisfaction. He wanted to fight, to lead his trained legionnaires against the enemy.

Early in February of 1779, Pulaski received exciting news. His legion was ordered south. Savannah, Georgia, had fallen to the British, and they were moving up the Eastern coast. The people of Charleston, South Carolina, felt they would soon be swallowed up by the enemy, and they called upon Washington for assistance.

Calling his legion to Lancaster, Pennsylvania, Pulaski mapped out the movement south. Anxiously he waited for Congress to appropriate another fifty thousand dollars for him to pay his men and to lure new recruits. As usual, the money was slow in coming. But there was no time to waste. Fortunately, there were men from Virginia and the Carolinas who offered maps and directions. After the recent experiences getting to Minisink, Pulaski appreciated having guides who knew the route.

Funds from Congress were still being delayed. But Pulaski could not wait any longer. Charleston needed help. The cavalry chief split his legion, sending some to Charleston to strengthen the forces there, others to Williamsburg, Virginia, to recruit new soldiers and to gather supplies. The bulk of his troops were dispatched to New York, to join General Washington.

Pulaski knew that it was essential to build up the strength of his horses. The winter months had taken its toll, and the cavalrymen's mounts were tired. Thankfully, wherever they went, the legion was welcomed by farmers grateful for added protection.

Pulaski remained in Lancaster as long as he could, waiting for the funds from Congress. He hated to rejoin his men without being able to pay their wages. Finally, he received thirty-five thousand of the fifty thousand dollars he was due. He could wait no longer. After sending a letter to Congress expressing his disappointment at the insufficient funds, Pulaski rode south to join his men. He caught up with his infantry in South Carolina. Now, the big question was, who would get to Charleston first—the American army or the British army? With a group of volunteer infantrymen, Pulaski set out for Charleston. Within a day, his cavalry caught up with them. As they neared Charleston, they sent scouts ahead. Happily, they learned the British had not reached the city yet, but they were on the way.

Outside Charleston, in a wooded swamp, Pulaski discovered a huge British company led by Gen. Augustine Prevost. Estimates put his number of soldiers at thirty-six hundred, while Pulaski had but a cavalry of three hundred. Most military leaders would never have attempted contact. Yet Casimir Pulaski welcomed such odds. His saber raised, his horse straining at the bit, the brave Pole led the way. "Charge!" he shouted, and his men echoed "Charge!"

The British soldiers were stunned. No action was expected until they reached the city of Charleston. Before they could aim their rifles or fire their pistols, the cavalry sliced and slashed their weapons away. Pulaski's victory thrilled the local Charleston militia, offering them new hope and faith.

But Charleston officials still pondered whether or not to surrender their city to the British. After all, no one wanted the buildings razed or burned. The people called their place "a jewel of the South," its pink-red clay buildings standing like handsome sentinels along wide streets that stretched to the clear blue of the bay area. A fire had devastated the city in 1740, while a hurricane had ripped countless buildings out of the ground twelve years later. With determination and dedication, the residents rebuilt, and now Charleston was the fourth largest city in the colonies with the people claiming to be more culturally refined than the folks of Philadelphia, New York, and Boston. No, the Charleston residents did not wish to risk having their beautiful city destroyed by invading soldiers.

As soon as Pulaski entered Charleston in early May, he headed to the assembly hall. His reputation as a brave revolutionary soldier was well known and further expanded by the introduction offered by Col. John Laurens. Laurens, son of the Continental Congress president and a notable soldier himself, proved a valuable ally. Pulaski's spoken English was still lacking, although he made up in gestures and movements what he lacked in vocabulary. He noted the arrival of "the finest cavalry and infantry soldiers ever created by God and man," and he said that more were on the way under the command of Gen. Benjamin Lincoln. "You have nothing to fear from the British," he declared, "and you have little to gain by turning over your city to them." Pulaski boldly promised to fight no matter what those assembled decided.

The officials rallied around Pulaski, pledging their support. As soon as Lincoln arrived with additional troops, Pulaski organized a new attack on British general Prevost. The weary leader had retreated south of Charleston to Beaufort Island where he hoped to shore up his injured soldiers and receive supplies by ship. Pulaski, too, headed for Beaufort Island.

Unfamiliar with the South, Pulaski underestimated the problems caused by deadly mosquitoes in the sticky swamplands of the area. Although his aides suggested turning back as the colonial soldiers suffered from the heat and fever, the Pole would not give up. He fell victim to the disease himself, yet he was not about to turn back.

Reaching Prevost's units, Pulaski led a charge on the rear guard. As usual, Pulaski's lead inspired his weakened troops. They wiped out those who fired on the colonists, took prisoners, and captured valuable supplies. Thanks largely to Pulaski's attacks, Prevost's command was reduced from thirty-six hundred to eight hundred.

News of Pulaski's victories spread from South to North, rousing the morale of the entire American army. The proud Polish patriot received a hero's welcome when he returned to Charleston. People lined the streets, shouting his name and cheering his men.

But the joyful cheers soon waned. The summer of 1779 proved a difficult time for Casimir Pulaski. He still suffered from the dreaded "swamp fever" he had caught during the campaign south to Beaufort Island. Pulaski spent many afternoon hours shaking violently from chills. Fever set in, and there were days when his life seemed in jeopardy. "He fights the illness like he fights the enemy," wrote Pulaski's faithful aide Capt. Paul Bentalou, "with the strength and power of a lion." Slowly Pulaski regained his health. Friends took him to the theater and symphony. Memories of long-ago days in Poland, of grand parties at the Winiary and the king's palace, returned. Pulaski decided that he would make Charleston his home after the war was over.

Whenever he could, Pulaski visited area hospitals, cheering up soldiers and aides. His cousin and Polish comrade, Lt. John Zelinski, lay in bed severely wounded, and Pulaski spent hours with him, recalling good times in "the old country."

Yet the Polish cavalry chief remained frustrated with the American Congress. As always, funds trickled in slowly, forcing Pulaski to pay many of his soldiers with apologies.

"You may call me a hero," he wrote to the government officials, "but you treat me like a beggar."

By early autumn of 1779, Pulaski grew eager for more action. Headquartered about fifty miles northeast of Augusta, Georgia, Pulaski and his men awaited news about the French fleet. An ally with the Americans against the British, the French government promised to send ships from the West Indies. Their destination? The Atlantic coastline off Savannah, Georgia. After seizing the city in December of 1778, the British had made it the capital of the royal government. Whoever won Savannah back for the Americans would be a true hero. The proud Pulaski longed for such a victory. He could hardly wait for the arrival of the French ships so he could get on with his dream.

Chapter Fourteen
Southern Sunset

Where were they? For weeks Pulaski and his men had waited for the French ships to arrive. Had they been caught in a sea storm and lost? Or perhaps there was no wind on the sea, and all the vessels lay silent and unmoving on the water.

At least the Southerners showed the kind of hospitality on which they prided themselves. They willingly shared their homes and food with the colonial soldiers. When Pulaski needed hay for his cavalry horses, the farmers accepted IOUs. Recruits signed up eagerly, bringing their own horses and rifles.

Finally, early in September of 1779, the French ships arrived off the coast of Georgia. Under the command of Adm. Charles d'Estaing, the collection of vessels included twenty-two first-class ships, two of them manned with fifty guns. Five thousand men accompanied the mission. With such a powerful blockade, there seemed little way for the British in Savannah to receive supplies from their own sea vessels.

Quickly the American military leaders sprang into action. They huddled together, studying maps of Savannah and the surrounding area. They decided to venture closer to the city. To get more information about the area, they sent Captain Bentalou to scout ahead by canoe and report back. It took him a full day to chart his observations. Once he had

surveyed the enemy's defensives, he hurried back to tell Pulaski. The captain did not get far. The impatient Pulaski and the rest of the American fighters had each taken the canoe trip themselves! Once he had spoken with Bentalou and had studied his jottings, Pulaski took off with a group of men. They scampered up the northern bluff of the city, surprised the guards there, and returned with them as prisoners. The amused Bentalou merely shook his head in disbelief.

But Pulaski was eager to find Admiral d'Estaing. All summer the Americans had waited for the French ships to arrive. Now that they were somewhere off the Georgia coast, there seemed to be no sign of the Frenchmen themselves.

Pulaski pushed his men farther, closer to the sea. He captured more British prisoners, some of them scouts and others merely unarmed workmen building an outpost. Soon the cavalry chief had more enemy prisoners than men in his own fighting force.

It was nighttime when Pulaski reached oceanside. There, like thousands of fireflies, twinkled a long line of campfires. Chopping waves had slowed the French landing. Pulaski rode his horse down the sand dune and into the camp. It was a relieved Admiral d'Estaing who ran to embrace his fellow European fighter.

Pulaski led d'Estaing to Greenwich on the Wellington River, some three miles south of Savannah where a headquarters post had been set up. Then Pulaski shared his maps and knowledge about Savannah. D'Estaing listened intently.

As he rode from the Greenwich headquarters, Pulaski felt comfortable. Between the American and French forces, surely the enemy could have little chance for holding Savannah.

But d'Estaing pulled a major surprise. Without telling the American military leaders, he sent word to the British officials in Savannah. Surrender, the French chief demanded, surrender at once.

The British leaders begged for time, twenty-four hours, and suggested a peaceful armistice for that time. D'Estaing agreed, not knowing the British were sending for reinforcements and building up their defensive positions.

Pulaski was furious when he heard about the armistice. The time for attack was now, he insisted to his aides. But Gen. Benjamin Lincoln did not agree. He voiced thought of a more peaceful blockade, cutting off the city from supplies on land or sea. Savannah could not last long without food, and lives could be saved.

The British refused to surrender. The French ships rolled into position and began bombarding the city. American and French infantry moved, surrounding Savannah, and began moving in.

Without warning, the skies opened, and rain poured down. It did little harm to the British who lay comfortably hidden under defensive installations. But the American and French soldiers suffered in the rivers of water. Dysentery, caused by spoiled rations, spread among the troops.

Drastic and immediate action was called for. At a meeting held the night of October 8, Pulaski was named to command both the American and the French cavalry. He proposed a plan that called for him to lead a daring charge into the midst of the strongest point of the British defensives, the right side. Other troops, appearing to attack the center and left points of the British defense, would also follow Pulaski on the right side. The enemy would be confused and try to split its troops.

It was a daring plan. Much depended upon its surprise value. Yet none of the American and French leaders noticed a man named Sgt. Maj. James Currie standing outside their tent. During the night, Currie left the camp and headed right to the British officials in Savannah. He shared the entire plan of attack.

Unknown to the Americans and French, it was the British who had the surprise in store the next morning. All their soldiers were in position. Each one knew the enemy plan.

As d'Estaing led his troops near the southern swamplands not far from Savannah, the British opened fire. Cannonballs and bullets ripped into the surprised soldiers, and those who were not shot, took off in wild panic. D'Estaing shouted orders, trying to rally his men back into order.

Leading his cavalry of two hundred men nearby, Pulaski was stunned to hear the explosions. He galloped to the hillside where he could see what was happening. The sight of French troops falling everywhere and scrambling for cover shocked him. Suddenly, he spotted d'Estaing. Before he could motion to the French admiral, the man fell to the ground, the victim of a British bullet.

Ignoring the danger, Pulaski snapped his reins and raced forward. His cavalry followed. Cannon exploded everywhere, a shower of cross fire rained among the men. Pulaski reached d'Estaing's side and ordered several soldiers to carry the officer's body to safety.

Another shot found its mark, this one in Pulaski's thigh. He jerked in his saddle, while still another ball caught him in the chest. He fell from his horse.

Captain Bentalou jumped to the ground to help his fallen commander. A bullet ripped into Bentalou's neck.

In all, the attack on the British October 9 lasted less than an hour. But when the bodies were counted, the French had lost over a thousand men, while the British counted one hundred and sixty-three casualties.

Taken to his tent, d'Estaing was treated by his own physician. The French admiral's injuries were not as serious as was initially thought. But Pulaski's proved to be worse. D'Estaing ordered his doctors to care for the cavalry chief. They recommended moving him to a nearby ship where it was cooler, and where there were no flies or mosquitoes.

When he regained consciousness, Pulaski looked into the face of his aide Bentalou. The captain's head was wrapped in bandages from his neck wound, but he insisted on staying close to his leader.

As the American brig *Wasp* rocked lazily in the water off the Georgia coast, highly skilled French surgeons worked desperately to save Pulaski's life. They removed one bullet, but another remained. The patient was too weak to undergo a second operation.

For two days Pulaski rambled on to his companion Bentalou. The Pole spoke of growing up at the Winiary, of his family, of his love for his faith. His fingers touched a medal of our Lady of Czestochowa he had pinned to his clothing. "Jesus, Mary, Joseph," he cried out, and then he was gone. Captain Bentalou wept at his commander's bedside. The date was October 11, 1779. Casimir Pulaski was thirty-two years old.

For three days the French ships had stood silently by as the doctors fought to save Pulaski's life. Now he was gone. His body, riddled with gangrene from his wounds, was quietly slipped into the sea as Bentalou and the crew of the *Wasp* watched. The afternoon's silence was broken by the sounds of the French cannons offering their final salute to Pulaski. Then the ships sailed homeward.

General Washington was visibly moved by news of Pulaski's death. "He was the most noble kind of hero," the Continental army commander said. "It is one thing to fight and to die for your country. It is quite another to fight and die for freedom itself."

With its ensign flying at half mast, the *Wasp* headed to Charleston. Word of Pulaski's death passed quickly among the city residents. Government officials called for a grand funeral and a day of "universal mourning."

The horse from which Pulaski had been shot followed the empty coffin in the funeral procession. Saddled and bridled, the handsome stallion carried the folded uniform in which the cavalry chief was struck down. Pulaski's sword, lance, and spurs sparkled in the afternoon sun. The crowd who joined the procession formed a line around the entire city of Charleston.

The funeral tributes to Pulaski brought tears to the eyes of many. Colonel Henry Lee of Virginia said, "Those who knew Pulaski intimately know the sublimity of his many virtues and the loyalty of his friendship."

As the funeral ended and the crowd started to disperse, a strange event occurred. Pulaski's horse momentarily broke away from the soldier who was leading it. Racing ahead several steps, the animal suddenly lifted its front legs high into the air.

"You could almost hear our leader's voice," Captain Bentalou wrote later. "The command of 'Charge!' seemed to float on the wind. Then it was over and the horse returned to his position. It was over."

Bibliography

Adams, Dorothy. *Cavalry Hero—Casimir Pulaski.* New York: P.J. Kennedy and Sons, 1957.

Alden, John Richard. *The American Revolution.* New York: Harper and Row, 1962.

Andrews, Wayne (editor). *Concise Dictionary of American History.* New York: Charles Scribner's Sons, 1961.

Army Times Editors. *Great American Cavalrymen.* New York: Dodd Mead and Company, 1964.

Billias, George. *George Washington's Generals.* New York: William Morrow and Company, 1964.

Ellis, John. *Cavalry: The History of Mounted Warfare.* New York: G.P. Putnam's Sons, 1978.

Ketchum, Richard M. *The American Heritage Book of the Revolution.* New York: American Heritage Publishing Company, 1958.

Manning, Clarence. *Soldier of Liberty—Casimir Pulaski.* New York: Philosophical Library, 1945.

Index